Hang in There, Mama!

Hang in There, Mama!

Encouragement and Advice for Moms Raising Teens and Beyond

Ali Flynn

A Wiley Brand

Copyright © 2025 by Ali Flynn. All rights reserved.

Published by John Wiley & Sons, Inc., Hoboken, New Jersey.
Published simultaneously in Canada.

ISBNs: 9781394296736 (Paperback), 9781394296750 (ePDF), 9781394296743 (ePub).

Except as expressly noted below, no part of this publication may be reproduced, stored in a retrieval system, or transmitted in any form or by any means, electronic, mechanical, photocopying, recording, scanning, or otherwise, except as permitted under Section 107 or 108 of the 1976 United States Copyright Act, without either the prior written permission of the Publisher, or authorization through payment of the appropriate per-copy fee to the Copyright Clearance Center, Inc., 222 Rosewood Drive, Danvers, MA 01923, (978) 750-8400, fax (978) 750-4470, or on the web at www.copyright.com. Requests to the Publisher for permission should be addressed to the Permissions Department, John Wiley & Sons, Inc., 111 River Street, Hoboken, NJ 07030, (201) 748-6011, fax (201) 748-6008, or online at www.wiley.com/go/permission.

The manufacturer's authorized representative according to the EU General Product Safety Regulation is Wiley-VCH GmbH, Boschstr. 12, 69469 Weinheim, Germany, e-mail: Product_Safety@wiley.com.

Trademarks: Wiley and the Wiley logo are trademarks or registered trademarks of John Wiley & Sons, Inc. and/or its affiliates in the United States and other countries and may not be used without written permission. All other trademarks are the property of their respective owners. John Wiley & Sons, Inc. is not associated with any product or vendor mentioned in this book.

Limit of Liability/Disclaimer of Warranty: While the publisher and author have used their best efforts in preparing this book, they make no representations or warranties with respect to the accuracy or completeness of the contents of this book and specifically disclaim any implied warranties of merchantability or fitness for a particular purpose. No warranty may be created or extended by sales representatives or written sales materials. The advice and strategies contained herein may not be suitable for your situation. You should consult with a professional where appropriate. Neither the publisher nor author shall be liable for any loss of profit or any other commercial damages, including but not limited to special, incidental, consequential, or other damages. Further, readers should be aware that websites listed in this work may have changed or disappeared between when this work was written and when it is read. Neither the publisher nor authors shall be liable for any loss of profit or any other commercial damages, including but not limited to special, incidental, consequential, or other damages.

For general information on our other products and services or for technical support, please contact our Customer Care Department within the United States at (800) 762-2974, outside the United States at (317) 572-3993 or fax (317) 572-4002.

Wiley also publishes its books in a variety of electronic formats. Some content that appears in print may not be available in electronic formats. For more information about Wiley products, visit our web site at www.wiley.com.

Library of Congress Control Number: 2025027928 (print)

Cover Design: Paul McCarthy

SKY10122325_071825

To my four girls

Without you, this book would not have been possible. Raising you through the hilarious moments of laughter and the heartbreaking moments of chaos and self-doubt have led us here today. Together we grew up and learned life lessons from one another, and I am so profoundly blessed to be your mom. Each of you have made me a better person, and I am so grateful to carry parts of you with me as I travel my motherhood journey. You are loved.

Motherhood is a journey, a beautifully imperfect step-by-step process that can be improved but never mastered. It's a journey within ourselves, one of humbling self-discovery. Motherhood is a time of healing, a time of growth, and a short moment in time in which we are blessed to walk alongside our growing child or children as they navigate their own paths of self-discovery.

Motherhood...

Fleeting moments whirling by causing a haze to gather as time moves forward.

Motherhood...

Moments which take our breath away and allow us to pause but not completely come to a stop.

Motherhood...

Breathtaking moments captured yet often dulled by the outside world creeping in.

Motherhood...

Precious moments holding on, dreaming, praying, loving, and always moving forward as life swirls around us and within us.

Motherhood...

Who knew it could be so profound?

Motherhood...

Who knew the love in our hearts would open up the floodgates to our souls?

Motherhood...

Who knew a fog of intense emotion would take over our entire body?

Motherhood...

The beautiful simple moments of a perfectly filled life.

The words of Ali Flynn are oxygen to a weary mom's soul.

No matter how long you've guilt-tripped yourself, neglected your needs, or abandoned your dreams, Ali offers us real hope. Through relatable struggles and heartfelt honesty, Ali gives guidance and permission to care for ourselves as we care for our kids.

—**Rachel Macy Stafford,**
*New York Times Bestselling Author
& Certified Special Education Teacher*

Contents

Introduction *xix*

Part I Motherhood   1

You Are Not Alone   6

I'm Not "Just a Mom"   8

Losing Myself or Letting Go?   10

Hope in the New Day   13

Being a Mama   16

Blessings Are All Around Us   19

Mistakes Happen   21

You Are Enough   23

A Mother's Love   26

Do You Love Yourself?   28

I Am More   31

Pottery Wheel Spinning   34

Lunchbox Love Letters   37

The Evolving Journey of Motherhood   41

Hang in There, Mama. You've Got This!   44

Step-by-Step   46

I Have A Secret   50

I Cried Today   53

Self-Love   56

This Is Motherhood   60

Little Pep Talks As I Walk   62

Now I Get It   64

It's a Marathon, Not a Sprint   67

I'm Worthy Too   70

Here's to You, Mama   73

A Mother's Hope   74

Would You Know?   76

Part II Raising Teens   81

Holding On While Shifting   86

Falling Short, Maybe Not   89

The Open Road   92

Tearful Smile   96

If Only I Knew   99

Our Teens Need Us   101

24/7   104

Patiently Waiting   106

A Mother's Warmth   108

Catch Me   110

Side-by-Side   112

Grace in the Dressing Room   115

Breathe, Mama   118

There, I Said It   120

Blooms of Life   123

Climbing Uphill   126

My Motherhood Journey   129

Remember When?   133

More Mistakes   137

Mama   139

Some Days Are Hard   141

One Rose and a Thorn   144

Lean In   146

Fighting Little Fires   150

A Peaceful Drive   153

Chaos and Truth   155

Decisions, Decisions   158

Don't Give Up On Me, Mama   160

Life Changes   163

Part III Letting Go   167

Last Moments   174

How Is Today Already Here?   178

Is My Heart Ready?   181

The Nest   183

Missing You   186

It's Hard to Let Go   190

I'm Trying   192

Always a Mom   195

Packed Bags   198

Goodbyes Are Hard   201

The Changing Season   204

Worn Out Shoes   207

Crying Over a Car   209

I'm Scared...   213

Luggage and Letting Go   216

Staying Strong   219

One of Those Moms   222

From Heartache to Happiness   224

Home   227

Broccoli   230

A New Season   233

What Do You Do?   236

The New Me   238

The Way Back Home   241

Empty Nest   243

To Go Back in Time   246

Coming Home   249

Acknowledgments   *255*

About the Author   *257*

Being a mom isn't about separating the woman you were before having children from the woman you are now.
It's about blending the two together, erasing the line separating them, and becoming who you are meant to be today, a beautiful balance of old and new woven intricately together creating a woman with a heart full of love.

Introduction

M*ama, you've got this!*
Do you sometimes feel alone as you travel your motherhood journey, feeling like you are the only one balancing the beautiful and difficult moments of motherhood that so often take your breath away, yet you wouldn't trade it for anything?

Do you feel lost within yourself and question who you have become while raising your kids yet cherish the family you have created and feel beyond grateful by the abundance of blessings more than anything in this world?

Well, after 21 years of being a mom, I just want you to know this…you are not alone.

As a mom, raising four daughters, I still find that I question myself every day. I know some days are simply hard; there are no other words for it, and I want you to know that if you are feeling this way too, you are not the only one. I am in the thick of this with you and along for the ride with you. This journey of motherhood has a lot of bumps in the road and many twists and turns, that's for sure, but I also want you to know that admitting this truth doesn't imply you are a bad mom. Rather, it makes you human.

The truth is we are not meant to be perfect, but for some reason, as mothers, we think we need to be. We are not meant to know exactly what to do in any given circumstance that comes barreling our way on our motherhood journey, and we are not meant to carry the load of everyone in the family. We are also not meant to take on every role in the family, and most certainly we are not meant to take this on all alone.

The best piece of parenting advice I ever received was to *be the mom my family needs me to be, not who others need me to be*, and I hold this as close to my heart today as the first day I heard it. I remember that evening, lying in bed, eyes wide open as I often do at 3 a.m. thinking about these words and saying it over and over again. . .*be the mom my family needs me to be, not who others need me to be*. This one sentence caught me off guard with how powerful it was, and as I digested this truth, I felt a change take over my body and heart, as a gradual sense of peace slowly washed over me. It was then and there that I made a vow to myself. I made a promise to myself, and my daughters, in the darkness of the night, and I have never looked back.

I finally stopped worrying about what others thought about my parenting and focused solely on my daughters. It didn't matter anymore what other moms were doing or what other people thought about my parenting skills. I needed to embrace this truth, hold on to it, and raise my girls by trusting my intuition and listening to my heart, as well as theirs. And then something profound began to happen. I transformed into being a mom listening to her heart, while not comparing myself to others, and accepting that the goal of perfection was never going to be attained, and I started to open up to other moms. I felt it deep in my bones to share this truth with other moms while also sharing who I was and how I was feeling as I traveled my motherhood journey.

Introduction

I became a mom who made mistakes and a mom who shared those mistakes.

I became a mom who admitted that being a mother is beautiful yet also extremely difficult at times.

I became a mom who recognized that we all have strengths and weaknesses, and it's okay to share those moments of weakness with one another.

In my early stages of motherhood I quickly realized that being a mom is not for the faint of heart no matter if you have one, four, or seven children. At one point in time I had newborn identical twins and two toddlers, all born within three and half years, and let me tell you our home felt as if a tsunami swept in most days in those early years. But with lots of caffeine, laughter, and huge doses of adrenaline I managed, along with my husband, to keep it together as best as we could, and I wouldn't alter one moment during this time. Even on the hardest of days, there was a sense of controlled chaos that I was able to embrace and a schedule that helped me move through the day according to what was needed to get accomplished while spreading large doses of love and countless amounts of giggles on to my girls. But some days I also felt that something was missing but couldn't quite grasp what it was.

As my girls got older, our vibrant home was filled with laughter and some tears, loud voices, and moments of pure silliness, and nowhere in this mix was perfection. We were a home where perfection simply didn't have prevalence, chaos took over out of the blue, and many emotions seeped out from all of us, but again I wouldn't change this for a moment even though some days were downright brutal. Because you see, Mama, it's within this messiness we learned about each other and grew up alongside one another. We learned about our strengths and weaknesses, how to love when it feels hard to love, and how to forgive. It's within the chaos we drew closer together as a family and learned how to dig deep. But I still felt a tug on my heart that a piece was missing, yet I couldn't put my finger on what it was.

As a mom, I had to suit up each morning with courage, patience, and a large dose of emotional stability while also being a caretaker, chef, driver, endless cheerleader and so much more. I thought I was prepared for all that motherhood and raising teens would entail since I was a former seventh grade teacher and I thought I had a toolkit filled to the brim with tips and tricks but being a mom is vastly different from being a teacher.

Preparing each day for the demands of motherhood isn't always easy, as you know, yet I often kept my feelings inside. I shared a decent amount of my feelings with those close to me but a lot of what I was feeling, especially when I was feeling "not good enough," I kept close to my core and hidden. I felt alone and embarrassed. The thoughts that woke me up in the middle of the night are exactly what I didn't share with the outside world because I felt that I couldn't or I would be viewed as less than.

Losing Yourself in Motherhood

As my girls got older and I was faced with raising four daughters, all in high school at the same time, with hormones surging throughout the house and emotions running wild, I truly never knew what was going to happen next. But I realized something about myself during this season of time. I needed to pause and tune in to my girls because if I didn't do that, I was possibly going to lose connection with my budding teen, and my home would become a battle zone where the world of mom and daughters collided. I needed to focus and do everything possible to remain connected to my girls as well as myself. I had to consistently go back to *be the mom my family needs me to be, not the mom others need me to be.*

But Mama, as my motherhood journey progressed, I realized being a mother didn't just entail being the mom my family needed me to be; it was also *being the woman I needed to be.* I found that as much as I would try to remain true to who I was as the woman I knew prior to having my kids, that woman slowly started to slip away, and that right there was the piece that was missing. I wasn't the mother I wanted to be some days because I was consumed with the stressors and the stigma of motherhood, and I surely wasn't the mom I envisioned I would be. I still fell into the trap that mothers are perfect. I still bought into the idea that moms don't make mistakes, everything runs smoothly, and we have to put on a happy face at all times, never showing or sharing our feelings or emotions. I had to keep going back again and again to the phrase I vowed to listen to each day, and I realized it wasn't just about raising my daughters; it was also about remaining true to the woman I was before becoming a mother and dig deep to find her again. *How could I be the mom I needed to be for my family if I wasn't the woman I needed to be for myself?*

One morning as the sun began to peek through the window at an ungodly hour, I realized something. Each day was on repeat: wake up, brush teeth, wake up the girls, start breakfast, laugh over something silly while eating Ritz crackers and peanut butter, take one sip of coffee, make lunches, more coffee, run out the door, do what I need to do that day to keep our home running as smoothly as possible, school pick up line, snack, maybe some tears from at least one child, running around like a mad woman to after school activities, endless orthodontist appointments, dinner, listening to as many stories about the day as possible, try to relax, bed time, repeat....

Where was I on this long day? The short answer was nowhere.

Years later, upon deeper reflection, I discovered the loss I felt. I woke up every day wondering how to make the lives of the people around me more fulfilled, and *I let go of me*.

As much as I thoroughly enjoyed being a mom I didn't set boundaries, and I was too emotionally available. I started going through the motions rather than living life each day. I didn't wake up refreshed, ready to take on the day, rather I was tirelessly traipsing through the day while still attempting to be the best mom I could be by putting on a smile, being silly, and finding little ways to laugh with my kids as we created a lifetime of memories.

Rediscovering Yourself

Upon further reflection, I recognized what was missing. *I let go of me*. I didn't like what I saw, and I knew it would take a lot of effort, but I mustered up the strength and reached deep into my soul and slowly started to find myself again. I gently traveled to the parts of myself I'd been missing, brushed myself off while being wrapped in a warm embrace, and invited myself back in again. I slowly started to find myself again.

I began to set aside little moments, snippets of time, dedicated to a run down a long country road, or sipping a chai latte at the local coffee shop gazing out of the window, or chatting with a friend honestly about this motherhood gig. I slowly began to emerge when I finally allowed the mom guilt to leave and the self-love to enter back in. Because here's the truth, Mama: caring

Introduction

for yourself isn't selfish. It is necessary in order to be the woman and mom you want to be.

Once I'd made this shift to allow self-love to be present once again and not simply drown myself into being a mom, I started living again. I slowly, and with some hesitation, attempted my best to let go of the mom guilt or at least some of it. I let go of the looming thoughts and stressors that burdened me in the midst of our daily lives. I stopped feeling selfish for the times I devoted to myself to make me happy, and I slowly started to find myself again.

I started living for my family as a whole, not just going about my day focused only on my children. For the first time in this long parenting journey, I lived for all of us collectively. And as I slowly started to find myself again, I became a woman filled with more joy to share with her children and herself. I felt filled up again as a human being, not simply a woman with the title of mom. I was so much more than that. Being a mom is my greatest blessing in life, but it's only one piece of who I am as I stare at my reflection every morning.

Hang in There, Mama

So many times along my motherhood journey when people would ask me how I was doing, my response was simply, "I'm hanging in there." I felt I couldn't say every day was amazing because then I was lying to myself and others about the hardships I was facing as I attempted to balance raising kids, being a mom, and remaining true to who I was as an adult woman, but I also couldn't say I was drowning because that feeling didn't consume me each day. So my simple mantra is what I held close to my heart, "I'm hanging in there," and I believed this truth to my core. I would say to myself during times of stress, "Hang in there, Mama. You've got this!" Because it was true, I was hanging in there through my kids navigating the stress of middle school friendships and the reality of feeling heartbreak when left out, academic pressure, and the dreaded comparison trap, but I was also hanging in there with my own emotional stress of feeling not good enough as a mom and constantly being filled up with self-doubt even though my smile said otherwise.

So Mama, if you can hold close to your heart the simple phrase, "Hang in there, Mama. You've got this!" you too may begin to feel more grounded as you navigate the many phases of motherhood. May you be filled up with words of encouragement through the many inspiring stories that I share to remind you that even on your hardest days there is always a glimmer of hope in tomorrow.

May you be reminded that we all fall short but through the raw words within my confessions you will feel less alone.

May you be reminded that we all have parts of ourselves that are difficult to admit but accepting this part of ourselves leads to the honest beauty within and one day our authentic selves as a woman and a mom will emerge.

May you be reminded that we all have ups and downs, life ebbs and flows, and our motherhood journey is rarely a constant but the love for your child never wavers.

And may you know that in those dark and lonely quiet moments when you feel that you aren't a good enough mom, know and believe that you are. As your trusted friend, I am right beside you wrapping you in love and comfort and reminding you of this truth.... You are an amazing mom.

Hang in there, Mama.
You've got this!
Love,
Ali

Motherhood is walking through many seasons which leave you breathless.

It's filled with moments of utter joy, devastating sorrow, and love that seeps out from the depths of your soul. Motherhood is the power of a woman unconditionally loving her children for a lifetime.

PART

I

Motherhood

The most sacred space I have in my heart is being a mother.

Introduction for Motherhood

Do you ever take a step back and look at your children and wonder "how am I so blessed?" These moments happen for me all of the time. Maybe it's when they come running into the house excited to share something with me, a spontaneous hug in the kitchen, or my first glimpse of them as they exit the airport after the many miles that college causes us to remain months apart. Mama, raising my girls is the most priceless dream I could have ever been blessed with and my greatest accomplishment in life and I can only assume one of yours too.

It's fulfillment beyond measure, beyond words, beyond time, and beyond love.
It's a dream I never let go of and relive each day with joy filling up my heart.
When I was younger and other dreams came crashing down or there were pivots and turns on my journey, being a mom always remained a constant and a dream I held on to, never letting go.

I have realized that motherhood fills my lungs with a breath that is so rich and fulfilling with adoration and devotion but it also ironically has the capacity to suck my lungs dry leaving me aching and alone wondering if I'm doing it right and some days it takes a toll on my heart.

Some days I feel lonely.
Some days I feel like I'm failing while everyone else is thriving.
Some days I feel like I can't manage everything on my plate.
Some days I'm anxious and just can't get it together.
And some days I'm left feeling worried and overwhelmed and I bet I can say that some days you feel this way too.

So if you are feeling this way at times just know, deep in your soul, that you are not alone. We all have days filled with beauty and chaos, epic fails, and huge wins. We all feel surrounded in love and then lonely at times. We are all on a journey through motherhood wondering if we are enough and guess what? You are enough.

If I have learned one thing on my motherhood journey, it's this…

It's time to release the days where I have self-doubt as a mom.

It's time to let go of mistakes made and focus on the lessons learned pushing me forward.

It's time to push aside all insecurities and allow the sun to shine, guiding me on my path.

It's time to gaze at the blooming flowers surrounding me and see the profound growth within myself as well.

It's time to listen to the chirping of the birds, outside my window each morning, before the sun rises and embrace their happy tune to begin the new day ahead.

It's time for a rebirth and a renewal, Mama.

It's time to become who we are meant to be, right here, right now, in this very moment.

It's time for new beginnings and anticipating what's to come.

We are all walking this journey of motherhood together, side by side, and the louder we cheer one another on and share with complete transparency and honesty, we have the ability for other moms to know that they too are not alone. As moms, we need each other. We need to hold on tight and support each other during the difficult times and the days filled with deep gratitude.

You are loved.
You are a wonderful mom.
You are not alone.

Being a mother unlocked parts of myself I never knew existed.

It opened me up to a love I never dreamed possible and a hopeful desire to make all things right. Motherhood breathed life into this heart of mine.

You Are Not Alone

To the mom feeling lost...
You are not alone.

To the mom feeling overwhelmed...
You are not alone.

To the mom simply going through the motions...
You are not alone.

To the mom struggling to hold back tears...
You are not alone.

To the mom feeling like she's not enough...
You are not alone.

To the mom who hasn't slept in months or years...
You are not alone.

To the mom giving her all each and every day...
You are not alone.

To the mom comparing herself to others...
You are not alone.

To the mom seeking out support and comfort...
You are not alone.

You Are Not Alone

To the mom in desperate need of a hug...
You are not alone.

To the mom needing a break to simply breathe...
You are not alone.

To the mom who has lost a part of herself...
You are not alone.

To the mom holding her kids tight in a world filled with chaos...
You are not alone.

To the mom struggling to hold on while letting go...
You are not alone.

To the mom wondering if she is doing enough...

You are enough.
You have always been enough.
You are not alone on your motherhood journey.

> *Motherhood is a beautiful chapter unfolding before me. Pages filled with many trials and tribulations, immense happiness, and profound love all wrapped up in one. Inner strength is stretched, patience is challenged, and love is unparalleled to anything else. Motherhood is a divine experience weaving together all of the pages of one lifetime.*

Reflection

A way I show myself I am enough...

I'm Not "Just a Mom"

I'm not "just a mom," I say to myself as I gaze at my reflection in the mirror.

I'm the one softly whispering words of encouragement into my child's heart each day, with the hope that she will always repeat these words as affirmations, especially on the days she feels lost and alone.

I'm the one offering tips and takeaways with the hope that each life lesson becomes the little voice she hears when she isn't quite sure what to do.

I'm the one making mistakes and owning up to them so one day she can be the one to courageously break the cycle and be a better version of a mother than I could ever be.

I'm the one giving endless hugs because that is what we know fuels our souls, sheds light on our darkest days, and allows us to feel loved and cherished.

I'm the one tenderly teaching her so one day she can reach deep inside, pull out all of the knowledge stored within, and change the world.

I'm Not "Just a Mom"

I am a believer of all things possible and a giver of hope.
I am a truth teller and memory maker.
I am warmth on a dark day and an embrace that takes away all of life's troubles.

I am a mother.
The greatest blessing one could ever receive.

I am not "just a mom."

I am a mother...
The most beautiful title bestowed upon me.

> *Some days, as moms, we need to hear we are doing something right. We need the gentle reminder that it's okay if the laundry still needs to be transferred to the dryer and the dishes need to be put away. We need to hear it's okay to feel like you need a break and through it all we need to hear, "You are doing a great job, Mama!"*

Reflection

Positive ways I remind myself that my title of mother shouldn't be taken lightly...

Losing Myself or Letting Go?

Do you ever feel a bit lost?

As if you are spinning around and around in circles on the merry-go-round but can't get off the ride?

Overwhelmed by the daily grind?

Not taking care of yourself, yet investing every breath into filling up someone else's day?

Exhausted by all of the little things, while the big things catapult you into complete oblivion?

Well, Mama, my tank was on the cusp of becoming barren, while clinging on to the hope of living life, rather than going through the motions.

And you know what I realized?

Some days I simply need someone to take care of me, and yesterday was one of those days.

Losing Myself or Letting Go?

So I invested time in myself and pampered myself a bit.

Mama, it doesn't matter what you choose to do; it's the art of doing something for you.
Not for your partner, not for your child, but for you.
Yes, you!

It doesn't matter if you are indoors or outdoors, if it's unembellished or profound, or if you are alone or surrounded by friends and family. It's the act of providing self-love and allowing others to love and care for you.

It has taken me a long time to realize self-care and self-love is not selfish. Rather, it is one of life's greatest gifts we can give ourselves.

Time to think.
Time to reflect.
Time to go deep and dig deeper.
Time to be still and love ourselves.

So today, it doesn't matter how you choose to give back to yourself as long as your soul feels full at the end of the day.

Is my soul grounded? Yes.
Is my soul thankful? Of course.
Is my soul blessed for these moments? Yes.

Can I adore my children and still take time for myself? You betcha!

Can I love my children while loving myself as well? Yup!

Can I cherish my children and not be considered selfish on the days I honor myself and grace myself with self-love through small pleasures? Yes!

Sweet Mama, take time for you.

You need to feel whole.
Your child needs you to feel satiated.
We need to deeply live life.
Truly live not just meander through it.

So Mama, let's vow to do one thing for ourselves today, no matter what that means for you. We deserve it!

Pinky promise?

> *I wish someone told me being a mom was hard so I didn't always think I had to be more than who I was in moments of self-doubt. I wish someone told me it's okay to lean on my partner and friends for support when life feels too much. I wish someone told me that being a mom would challenge me in ways I never expected and that it's more than okay to have days where I need to take a break and refuel my soul.*

Reflection

One thing I will do for myself today...

Hope in the New Day

As the morning sun gently cascades the bed and the flickering light washes over me, I am reminded of the hope in the new day.

Hope holds on to my hand letting me know I'm not alone on my journey of motherhood.

Hope sends soft whispers, when I feel broken down, reminding me tomorrow is just around the bend.

Hope embraces me, guiding me to inhale, exhale, and breathe.

Hope nourishes and refuels my soul when my weary heart is tired.

Hope restores my faith in knowing my path is guided by those I birthed.

Hope reassures me I'm not the only one.

Being a mom is hard.
Sometimes it's really hard.

But if we hold on, for the hope of tomorrow, many blessings will come to light.

As we travel the very bumpy road of motherhood, we need to remind our sisters, friends, and neighbors to hang on when raising our children drags us down and challenges come knocking on our door.

We need to remind one another some days are extraordinary and billowing with elation around every bend, while other days the twists and turns of life cut deep to the core and an ounce of patience is almost too hard to find.

But through it all, if I pause long enough, I will hear the subtle whisper of hope gently reassuring me to, "Hang in there, Mama."

Hang in there, Mama...
as your tween seeks independence but clings tightly to childhood, not knowing which path to choose as emotions run wild.

Hang in there, Mama...
as your teen spreads their wings, soaring in directions you never imagined while soaking in the bittersweet moment of letting go.

Hang in there, Mama...
as the adult before you searches for further independence and clarity but still has the soft giggle of the toddler you once held in your loving arms.

Our child is the hope that offers us peace.
Our child is the blessing that brings us to our knees.
Our child is the gift that reaches into our souls and changes us.
Our child is the truth that we share with full transparency.
Our child is the joy that allows expectations to be lost.
Our child is our heart overflowing with love.

This is motherhood.
Motherhood is a place of grace.
Motherhood is self-discovery.
Motherhood is a rebirth.
Motherhood is warmth and compassion seeping out each day.
Motherhood is love.

So as I travel this motherhood journey,
I take pause in knowing I'm not alone and hold tight to the many blessings the whispers of hope offers.

My eyes may be weary but the cascading light, in the early morning, nourishes my soul.

The light reminds me, yet again, as I breathe in and say a silent prayer of thanks, the hope in today will carry me through to the many tomorrows.

The hard days will move along, teaching us and guiding us, as the many blessings soothe our souls.

> *May the blessings of today fill my heart with hope for the new day tomorrow and all the many days to come. May my heart find stillness within the silence knowing that I am enough.*

Reflection

A few simple things that offer me hope. . .

Being a Mama

Being a mama is holding you, for the first time, and losing my breath.

Being a mama is loving so hard it leaves an ache on your heart.

Being a mama is knowing life is precious and butterfly kisses are powerful.

Being a mama is holding onto each word and memorizing your voice.

Being a mama is embracing today, holding onto the past, and longing for the future.

Being a mama is trying to soothe your soul as tears stream down your face.

Being a mama is investing it all for their future self.

Being a mama is holding hands tightly knowing one day you will have other hands to hold.

Being a Mama

Being a mama is having your heart broken over and over again.

Being a mama is joy filling your soul at the sound of your sweet laughter.

Being a mama is a quiet understanding that sleep will never be the same.

Being a mama is feeling overwhelmed while trying to be everything to everyone.

Being a mama is loving hard each day, the good, the bad, and the ugly.

Being a mama is exhaustion taking over while mustering up every ounce to listen some more.

Being a mama is silently sacrificing the very last cookie.

Being a mama is loving you over and over again.

Being a mama is beautiful and brutal.

Being a mama is hugging you and feeling peace wash over my soul.

Being a mama is unwavering love, unconditional support, and a never ending need to feel your warmth.

Being a mama is a blessing each day not taken for granted.

The intricate tapestry of a mother's life is a profound journey creating her legacy. A legacy that will span generations to come wrapped up in her love, resilience, and strength and what a gift this is to treasure over and over again.

Reflection

One thing I'm proud of as a mom. . .

Blessings Are All Around Us

Do you ever just take a moment and step back and say I am blessed?

The other day I was caught off guard when I took a step back and paused rather than reacted. I was hot and bothered, arms loaded up with groceries, a million things on my mind and I walked into a house with dirty dishes in the sink, leftover food on the kitchen island covering the entirety of it, and multiple teens who had no idea I even walked in the room.

I was spent.
I was exhausted, and I was feeling overwhelmed.

I put my bags down, walked back out to the car to gather the second load of groceries, turned my face to the sun and inhaled a breath of fresh air to carry me through this moment of overwhelm.

I assumed I was walking back into complete utter chaos, and to my surprise I walked into four daughters unloading bags, creating their own system of putting items away, reorganizing the snack cabinet, and everyone seemed to have a role.
Country music was blasting, windows were open, and they turned the chaos, my chaos, into a blessing.

As moms, we are surrounded by chaos so many hours of the day, and I think we often forget to have gratitude for this beautiful life with our children. We are consumed with taking on the physical load of caretaking and getting our kids from place to place and the emotional load our kids carry around as it takes over us and begins to truly suck the life out of us. And so often we forget about the beauty within it all. We forget how beauty is found within the mess, within the dirty dishes, and food all over the place. We forget there are blessings within our home that have nothing to do with perfection. It's simply blessings within the ordinary moments of life that we share with our kids.

So Mamas, the next time you are feeling the stress of motherhood take over, pause.
This pause is life-changing. It slows us down physically, it naturally slows our heart rate, and it allows us to witness the many blessings in our life that sometimes we just don't even see.

Those blessings, those moments, that is what fills our souls when we are feeling weary and tired and worn out. Those little moments are what allows us to move forward and not feel like we are drowning. Because you see, when we allow our beautiful blessings to take over we can be the mom we always dreamed of being.

> *Without pause, my children are my greatest blessings in life. A gift I am blessed to unwrap over and over until I take my very last breath.*

Reflection

One thing that made me feel blessed today...

Mistakes Happen

I will make mistakes, and I will continue to mess up today, tomorrow, and many days to come.
I am human, and I have to be okay with mistakes.
I don't mean to nit-pick at every little thing, but sometimes I simply can't take the messy room, not lending a helping hand, and the way everything is left until the last minute. It makes me feel a bit off balance and downright uncomfortable... I'm human.

I will make a bunch of errors.
I will have a lack of patience at times.
And sometimes I may even lack engagement...I'm human.

But I'm trying.
Everyday I try...

I try to provide a home filled with love and compassion, while offering support and comfort.
I try to laugh, belly laugh, each day... but lately that has been a bit hard.
So yeah, I have been making a lot of mistakes, but I'm learning... I'm human.

That handbook on motherhood?

Nope, it still doesn't exist. . . . so I will continue to make mistakes as I navigate being a mom.
But each night, as I collapse onto my bed even on the hardest of days, my heart is full knowing these four things.

Our home is filled with:
Grace
Love
Forgiveness
Optimism

Mistakes are forgiven with grace which only lends way to the light. A light that can always be found, even on the darkest of days. Mistakes happen. . . I'm human.

> *My mistakes don't define me. They allow me to learn and grow in order to become the mom I need to be for tomorrow and the many days ahead.*

Reflection

A mistake I have made that I'm not proud of. . . .

You Are Enough

You are enough...
You are beautifully perfect, don't ever let anyone crush your remarkable spirit.
Don't listen to the voices saying you are not good enough.
Don't listen to the voices saying you are not the right mold.
Don't listen to the voices, echoing in your head, saying you need to be more.
You are beautifully perfect.

Don't listen to the chaos of negativity pulling you under.
Don't listen to the toxicity emanating from the mouths of those who are weak.
Don't listen to those who find comfort in tearing you apart.
You are beautifully perfect.

Listen to your heart, the piece that elevates you and raises you up, encircling you in pure happiness.
Listen to your soul, the depth of your core, that fills you up with passion.
Listen to your inner voice, calling out your name, telling you that you are enough.
You are beautifully perfect.

Don't listen to the voices dragging down the spirit within you that searches for a brighter tomorrow.
Don't listen to the voices surrounding you, making you question your worth, physical beauty, and innermost self.
Don't listen to the voices that tug at your persona, forcing you to analyze every fiber of your being.
You are beautifully perfect.

Listen to what you know to be true and always remain loyal to who you are.
Listen to your heart, the one guiding you forward along your intimate journey of life.
But don't listen to the nonsense riddling your brain with lies.

You are enough.

Your love, your patience, unlimited words of encouragement.
Your hard work, your empathy, your grace.

You are enough just as you are and don't ever allow anyone to question your worth as a mother.
You are fierce.
You are strong.
You are loved.

We all make mistakes.
We all say things we wish were unspoken.
We all wish to go back in time and do things differently.
So let's give ourselves grace.

Grace to know we are human.
Grace to know that through our mistakes, we still love our kids.

You Are Enough

Grace to know what is tugging at our soul will work out.
Grace to know there is a new day.
Grace to know what we are doing each day matters.

You are enough.

> *Motherhood is not one size fits all. It's our own unique path. A path that deserves to be honored, nourished, and enriched with each new day. It's valuing the needs of your family while remaining true to who you are while acknowledging you are the exact mother your children need.*

Reflection

One way I show myself grace...

A Mother's Love

Each day I am reminded of what it means to truly love...
Unconditional love, at its finest.
I'm blessed to love through the sticky days and the days filled with glory.
I'm blessed to love through the messy days and the days with barely any imperfections.
I'm blessed to love while in a state of not knowing and in all of the perfectly organized, laid out plans types of days.

I question a lot...
I perseverate a lot...
My mind wonders a lot...

My love for my children is fierce.
It is never second guessed or thought about with doubt.
My love doesn't bring an ounce of anxiety or fear of failure.

My love simply brings on a sense of peace and security.
A security within myself, knowing my love doesn't waver...
not yesterday,
not today,
and not tomorrow.

A Mother's Love

This is a beautiful gift bestowed upon me...
to love unconditionally while wrapping my children in a warm embrace.
May they feel my love emanating through their souls daily,
every ounce of my love traveling within their hearts...
Yesterday, today, and all of their tomorrows.

A mother's heart holds the many blessings of her children for a lifetime and beyond.

Reflection

A moment my love endured over everything else...

Do You Love Yourself?

Do you love yourself?
Really love yourself?

It's hard some days, I get it, especially on days when all of the kids are home, we have our own work to accomplish for a big meeting, laundry to fold, and the list of all of the things that have to get done is a mile long.

We have all of these lists of things to do or others to take care of and all of those items do need to get checked off the list but let's think about something. . .

What about if today,
we add *ourselves* to the to-do list?

Sounds crazy right?!

But seriously, Mama, what if we became one of those items on the list, and we can't go to bed until it is accomplished?

Imagine finding one way each day to give ourselves love?

A time set aside to honor our needs and time to care for and cherish ourselves, not just today, but all of the days ahead.

A time to pay attention to filling up our cup with happiness and not expecting someone else to create our joy and a time to fall in love with ourselves over and over again.

Mama, when we have those moments of self-doubt,
where we want to pull ourselves down about all we didn't do today, or make a sarcastic remark about the new weight gain, let's remember that we are the model for our children and how we want them to love themselves.

Or the times we are hard on ourselves for not knowing something and our anxiety spikes or the times we rip ourselves to shreds for not being a perfect person,
let's remember our kids are hearing this negative self-talk.

We need to love ourselves with a depth that is so deep, it makes a profound impact on our children.

If we don't model self-love then who will?

So today, let's add a new bullet note to our to-do list,
It's just going to say, *me*.

Will it be enjoying a cup of tea while my girls binge watch Netflix and share with them how I'm going to take a few minutes alone, while they are busy?

Or maybe it's praising myself three times today about a job well done, and having the kids hear the praise and positive talk.

But one thing is certain, today, there will be a check mark next to ME before my head hits the pillow tonight.

> *Offering myself a dose of self-love each day is one of life's greatest gifts. It's a time for renewal and growth and a time to refuel my soul. It's a time to reflect on becoming the woman and mother I hope to be. It's a time to cherish who I am, my passions, desires, goals, and dreams. It's a time to wrap myself in love and embrace myself for who I am.*

Reflection

A few simple ways I show myself self-love. . .

I Am More

I am more...
I am more than a food shopper, driver to all activities, and entertainer of all kinds.
I am more than a gourmet chef, cleaner of dirty laundry, and bed maker.

I am more than a reminder to use the inhaler, listener at all times, hair braider, dishwasher emptier, and buyer of all school supplies.

I am more than hugs, snuggles, and goodnight kisses.
I am more than a mom.

I am more.
I am me.

I am a lover of meandering dirt roads, quiet sunsets on the bay, sand covering my coral painted toes, a run in the early morning, the ocean breeze, and laughter filling up my house.

I am more.
I am me.

I am a woman who loves browsing a small bookstore without a time limit, beautiful and unique stationery, iced tea, a cozy blanket nestled under my chin, hydrangeas and tulips, and the sun shining as I chat with friends.

I am more.
I am me.

I am comfortable in my quiet space, and happy in the company of others, a lover of listening to jazz music in a small bar, taking photographs, holding my daughters' hands, whispers late at night, a cup of tea in the early morning gazing out of the bedroom window, a kiss on my forehead from my husband, a beautiful cheese platter and glass of wine, and a lover of who I was as a little girl. . . Always outside riding my bike or swimming, laughing with friends sometimes snarky with a dash of sweetness, always thinking of those less fortunate, a lover of hard work, loyalty and truthfulness and the simple things.

I am more. . .
but sometimes it's hard to find when burdened by the other stuff.

But for now, I am being called by a voice downstairs to drive someone somewhere and maybe being the driver isn't so bad, as I listen to their stories and Zac Brown Band on the radio with the windows down and my hair blowing in the wind.

It is hard at times when I feel I have lost what I am more than. . . but then I hear their voices and realize this is my true love. The girls I am looking at, their whole being, innocent and wild, growing up in front of me, making the same mistakes I have made or doing the opposite and teaching me.

They are my more.

I Am More

They are my safe place and soft landing place.
They are who I admire and who I yearn to learn from.
They are my go-to when laughter needs to fill up my weary soul.

It's letting go of feeling incomplete along my journey, as one woman, and embracing how together we are more.
Together we are intertwined in a love molded by deep roots forever connecting us as a family while offering the gift of feeling more than enough each and every day.

Being a mother transforms your life as you revisit parts of yourself left behind while holding tightly to the new moments of self-discovery.

Reflection

A few ways I have grown as a mother...

Pottery Wheel Spinning

Today I am not myself.
I feel lost.
I feel consumed by stress.
I feel like I'm failing in motherhood.

Have I created enough core memories with my kids?
Have I fulfilled their desires and dreams?
Have I inspired them enough to believe in the belly of their soul they will make a mark on the world?

The what ifs, could'ves, would'ves, should'ves take over as I sit in the quiet car waiting for my daughter to exit the door of the building. These thoughts wrap themselves around me and suffocate me...and then my daughter, wearing mustard yellow jeans and braids, opens the car door smiling ear to ear and the overwhelming thoughts leave my mind as quickly as the car door closes. She wears a quiet grin filled with pride, and there is an emotion seeping out of her I have never witnessed before. She carries a strength deeply rooted with confidence creating an energy and spirit that takes over her as she exhales a beautiful sigh, releasing all of the air inside of her.

As we drive home, windows down, listening to her favorite songs she has on repeat, I slowly begin to let go of my thoughts swirling around in my head and simply let go.

With joyful tears in her eyes and a quiet anticipation wondering what I will think, she begins to reach into her bag and slowly share with me the many pieces of pottery she has created this season.

As I gaze at her before me, she is confident and secure filled with a sense of resilience and strength to never give up.
She is comfortable in her failures knowing they become moments of learning.
And a beautiful sense of peace simply washes over me.

So as my girl shows me the many bowls she has molded and created using her own delicate hands covered in clay and water, I realize something, and a new emotion creeps in and takes over me. Just like the hands of my girl molding her bowl or vase, as the pottery wheel spins, she decided if she is going to allow the pedal of the wheel to take over or if she would ease into it slowly and follow the lead of her hands on the journey of her creation.

It's not very different from being a mom. . . ..
Through failures and mistakes, things falling apart and crashing down, to feeling lost and spinning around and around, there is beauty. There is beauty that rises up within.
So today, I'm following the lead of my heart as I travel my motherhood journey, not looking back or ruminating on all that could have been different but rather I'm embracing the mother I am today, flaws and all.

Being a mom is simply breathtaking. It's filled with compassion, forgiveness, heartache, and beauty all wrapped up in the one precious gift we call motherhood.

Reflection

A way I'm accepting and embracing myself today for who I am. . .

Lunchbox Love Letters

For years, I wrote what I liked to call "lunchbox love letters" as my little way of reminding my girls how loved they were when at school. It was a way to reconnect or share my heart on the days the early morning just became too hectic to talk and slipped away from us before rushing out of the door.

Mama, let me explain, lunchbox love letters weren't carefully scripted or edited. It was simply what was on my heart, in that very moment, and a tradition I hope my girls will carry with them as they grow older.

As my teens entered middle school, though, I questioned if I should still write lunchbox notes, and I decided I was going to see what happened and take it day by day. These notes weren't daily or weekly, and there was really no set schedule. It truly happened when one of us needed more connection, I had a pen handy at 7 a.m., or I felt their heart could use a little encouragement.

Most days my girls didn't mention the note propped against the white napkin or sweet treat, but one day a friend of my daughter's who was sitting next to her was curious and asked, "What does your mom write?" I'm not sure what my daughter shared with her friend, but I know she wanted her to have a note the following day to know how it feels. Right there my mama heart melted a bit.

You see, I assumed these notes were considered annoying when middle school and high school came about, and some days I even refrained from writing them to not be a pest, but I realized in this moment my little lunchbox love letters meant more than I knew to my high school daughter.

Mamas, as we know the teen years are hard. It's a time filled with challenges and arguments, eye rolls, and sighs of frustration. It's a time where our teens are seeking independence but so desperately want to hold tight to their childhood, and all too often we don't know what the morning will bring as they venture into the kitchen to grab a quick bite to eat.

But as the morning dew gently covered the lawn and the sun peeked through the oak trees the following morning, I wrapped up a brownie and placed on top of it a yellow note with her friend's name written on it and a simple message saying, "Have a good day."

You see, Mama, it's the little things for me.
It's treating my kids' friends as one of my own.
It's holding close to my heart something that is important to them and hoping they feel loved by another mom, knowing so many people love them for who they are, the magical human they are branching out and becoming.

If 10 seconds of reading a small note can possibly change the course of the day for someone, then I will continue writing lunchbox love letters for as long as I possibly can. As my kids grow older and leave home, the lunchbox love letters may be replaced with messages of love in the mail or via text messages but one thing will always remain the same. . .lunchbox love letters will forever connect our hearts to one another.

As a mother, I'm far from perfect, but I always hope my kids feel my love surrounding them because this right here means everything to me.

Reflection

A special something I do for my kids that I hope will continue on. . .

Motherhood is feeling like you have given your all to then dig deep and find the strength to give some more.

The Evolving Journey of Motherhood

When I look back at myself as a young, new mom, I had so many visions of what my motherhood journey would be like, maybe you have this thought too.
I thought I had it all figured out, but I didn't.
I never thought I would lose my cool.
I never thought I would yell.
I never thought I would look into my child's eyes and feel such frustration at times.
But I do.

I thought life was going to be easy.
I thought each day was going to be filled with stickers and lollipops and rainbows.
I thought it was skipping down the street holding hands forever.
I never thought I would not be fun and silly.
I never thought I would have words escape my lips only wishing I could take them back.
I never thought I would get into heated arguments.
But I do.

I thought our biggest stressor was always going to be which flavor of ice cream to choose.
I thought I was always going to feel enough each day.

I thought I was going to live a life with no regrets.
I never thought I would have to search to find the adult version of me.
I never thought I would lose so much sleep.
I never thought I would cry this much.
But I do.

I thought swinging high in the sky was going to last forever.
I thought I was always going to have more time or maybe I thought time didn't move as fast.
I thought I was always going to solve problems with a hug.
I never thought some days I would dream of being left alone.
I never thought I would be blamed for so many things.
I never thought I would feel unprepared for this role.
But I do.

I thought life was going to be easy.
I thought running on empty was going to make things right.
I thought I was going to enjoy every waking moment.
I never thought I would come face to face with moments which made my knees crumble to the floor.
I never thought I would need to fill up my cup with my own dose of self-love, since I would eventually be empty.
I never thought I would have so many challenging days.
But I do.

Being a mom is beautiful but I wish someone told me there were also going to be some really difficult days.
There would be days which would take my breath away when I was feeling scared, at a crossroads, or alone.
But there would also be glorious days where my breath was lost by simply gazing into the eyes of my child and knowing the world is a better place.

Mama, if you too ruminate on these thoughts also at 3 a.m., because why wouldn't we overthink all of these things at such an ungodly hour in the wee hours of the night, just know in your heart that your concern and worry alone makes you a good mom. We all need the little reminder that what we thought we would be like as mom is nearly impossible to imagine since every second of every day is new for all of us. As moms, we don't know what to expect or what we are doing and it's important to keep that in the forefront of our minds. We are moms, present in the moment, taking life as it comes at us, and with the strength of a mother being the very best mom we can be for our kids.

> *I may not be a perfect mom or know how to fix everything that is pressing on my child's heart but I do know my love and encouragement will never waver and this is a promise I hold close to my heart. My love is a constant that will never end.*

Reflection

One thing I never thought I would do as a mom. . .

Hang in There, Mama. You've Got This!

Mama,

If today you woke up feeling defeated before breakfast, hang in there.

Maybe tomorrow by breakfast you will have a renewed spirit from a good night's sleep.

If today you are missing your college kid, hang in there.

Maybe tomorrow you are able to, once again, reconnect while cherishing beautiful memories.

If today you are laughing side-by-side with your teen which then abruptly leads to an argument, hang in there.

Maybe tomorrow the laughter comes back in full force.

If today you feel defeated while trying to connect to your teen, hang in there.

Maybe tomorrow your teen will plop down next to you chatting and ask you to pick up some take out together, while blasting music in the car and continuing the conversation.

If today you feel the weight of motherhood on your shoulders, the house responsibilities, listening to everyone's needs, and providing unconditional emotional support, hang in there.

Maybe tomorrow a friend will reach out to lift some of your burdens, knowing as a mom, sometimes we all need a break.

If today you feel your tank is a bit empty, hang in there.

Maybe tomorrow reach out for a loved one's hand and be honest, truly honest, and share how you need to be fueled up again and again.
If today you feel a deep rooted change needs to happen in your life, hang in there.
Maybe tomorrow the path ahead will be clear for you to create the changes you are seeking.
So on the days you may lose your breath, as you feel suffocated by life encompassing you, take pause, inhale, exhale, breathe, and hang in there.

> *Becoming a mother changes you. It reveals parts of yourself you never knew existed and opens up emotions you have never felt before. It's a journey filled with learning, healing, and tremendous growth that humbles you. Motherhood is breathtakingly beautiful and heavy at times, yet when intertwined together creates an unimaginable love to last a lifetime.*

Reflection

A way I offer myself grace even when things are hard. . .

Step-by-Step

I am rarely by myself, and if I happen to be, it is usually to use the restroom, shower, or on my way home after driving one of my four girls to a friend's house.

But last week I went snowshoeing alone.
Deep in the woods.
Alone...

It took me some time to settle in and stop worrying a bobcat was going to jump out and attack me, but I kept moving forward.

Step-by-step, I gained more confidence and left my fears behind.

Alone...
for the first time in a long time...

So there I was, alone in the woods.
Alone with my deepest thoughts.
Alone with the quiet and the sunlight peeking through the trees creating the most glorious shadows.

And as I walked along, listening to the snow crunching beneath my feet, I recognized that I truly wasn't alone and an inner peace embraced me.

Step-by-Step

There I was, trudging through the pathway of white, in all of my fullness.
This alone time was a gift as I was wrapping myself up in self-love and providing a space to reflect and grow.

Who knew just a short three mile snowshoeing trek could open up my heart to hearing and seeing new parts of myself...

Who knew the quiet and solitude would allow inner conversations to emerge and come to light...

And who knew being alone could feel so magical after so many years of always having my girls near me.

But maybe that's it right there...

Maybe being alone is exactly what I needed in order to find more growth within... to strive to be a better mom and to think through things, really think, not the kind of thinking that gets done in between loads of laundry and emptying the dishwasher.

And what I realized is this...
I am blessed to never feel alone, even when one set of footprints, my own, trails behind in the snow.

You see friends, this mama of four, will always see six sets of footprints trailing behind and what a blessing that is today and all the days moving forward.

Our family footprints are a given. There is no doubt that the love and support of my family encourages, inspires, and moves me along.

So all of this alone time got me thinking. . .

My oldest will be making her trek along a new path when she embarks on her college journey in the Fall.

She may have moments where she feels alone.
She may feel alone in the evenings when her dorm room is quiet and miss our bustling home, filled with high-pitched laughter, screams of frustration, and some tears.

She may feel alone as she walks across a campus busy with other students but miss holding her sister's hand.

She may feel alone when she grabs a quick granola bar on the way to class rather than sharing her to-do list with me, as she looks on while I make her an egg sandwich.

But maybe being alone is just what she needs. . .

Maybe being alone allows the quiet to seep in and feel blessed for the billowing laughter that wrapped her up each day in love.

Maybe being alone allows a sense of solitude to embrace her soul, while remembering a sense of peace from each hug.

But as this heart of mine gets used to being more alone among the world of raising teenagers, I can only wish for my sweet girl to also know, even on the days she feels alone, there are always six sets of footprints trailing behind, supporting every part of her being.

Our family footprints will forever trail behind each and every one of us, making imprints along our unique paths of life.

No one prepares you for how hard the mental load of being a mom can be. It's a time filled with heartache and constantly questioning if you're doing the right thing. It's a time where you need to give yourself loads of grace and time to sit within your thoughts because this is all new.
Finding yourself is a part of the journey.

Reflection

A few ways I have found comfort within and have grown as a mom...

I Have A Secret

I have a secret to share and maybe you do too. . .

Some days I fall into the comparison trap.

I start comparing myself to my friends, neighbors, and family members but I'm trying my very best to stop.
Even though I know this is unhealthy and I try my hardest to not fall down this path, some days it's just inevitable, it happens.

Once I start comparing though I fall into a downward spiral. I feel as if I'm falling into a bottomless space of feeling not good enough and I get trapped there in the darkness.

But, Mama, while I was walking today, along the back dirt country roads near my house, a reality took my breath away and made me stop, full stop, which rarely happens for me. A pressing thought came over me and quietly spoke to me, nudging me to acknowledge that I need to change.

I need to stop measuring myself against other moms.
I need to stop this tug-of-war where I am my own worst enemy.
I need to end the sleepless nights, perseverating on my mistakes that suck out every ounce of confidence that I may have for myself.

I need to begin to believe that I'm a mother who wakes up each morning as the sun peeks through the shades and offers a clean slate each day for her children and what a gift that is to provide unconditionally.

I'm a mother who shows her flaws and shares her deepest insecurities about life and I'm a mother who loves fiercely with her whole heart. I'm a mother who doesn't need to compare herself to anyone yet continues to but a shift needs to take place in order to move ahead confidently.

So as I continued to meander along the dirt road, I couldn't push aside this one thought that kept coming up over and over again reminding me that change can happen.

Just as the dry dirt covers my white sneakers and my vision is often blurred as a car speeds by pushing the dust into the air, once the dust settles, the dirt is always wiped clean revealing the white shoes once again and I faithfully always find my way.

You see, Mama, I have realized that motherhood is the same. I have moments of clarity where the dust settles and then the next moment I can't find my way but just as the dust swirls through the air, as a mom, I often spiral trying to make sense of it all and not get lost in the whirlwind.

I have moments of pure chaos where I think I am the only one in the mess and times of unity where I know I have a support system pushing me through.

I have times of clarity believing, with great confidence, that how I'm raising my teens is spot on and other times where my heart is troubled, my insecurities take over, and I wonder if everyone else has it together but me.

But today, as I walked I made a promise to myself.
Today and moving forward, I will accept myself for who I am. A mom who confidently loves her children and believes that I am more than enough. And maybe, just maybe, you will too.

> *When you begin to second guess your worth just remember you are everything to your children. You are the person who fills them with hope when they are down and the light carrying them through on their darkest days. Your love is not replaceable and you, Mama, are irreplaceable.*

Reflection

A way I am going to start to accept myself for who I am. . .

I Cried Today

OK, I'll admit it. I cried a lot today. I mean a lot.
Mama, does this ever happen to you? Where you feel a loss of control as emotions seep through every cell of your body? Where you wonder if this is going to last forever and you question if you can even handle the emotional load of it all?

I don't know what took over me. I'm usually not much of a crier unless I get so angry it makes me cry. I'm not a mom who cries at commercials or cheesy movies or even sad love songs, but today I cried.
Maybe it's all the years of not crying that finally led to those tears reaching in and exposing itself.
Maybe it's thinking about my girls and their childhood.
Maybe it's thinking about how my daughter turned 21 and wondering where the time has gone?
Maybe it's my twins, hitting the submit button on their college application knowing they too are leaving the nest.
Maybe it's knowing my other girl has big hopes and dreams and will follow her heart wherever it leads her.
Or maybe it's recalling the countless hours listening to hot cross buns on the recorder, clarinet, and the flute.
Maybe it's the art projects still taking over numerous cabinets within our home because I just can't part with them yet. I'm not

ready to let go of the handprint that's dons every Mother's Day card.
Maybe it's running into our all-time favorite third-grade teacher, at a local farm, and sitting down reminiscing at how far all of my girls have come.
Maybe it's wondering why I was so hard on them when they clearly had it all together or why I was equally hard on myself never feeling enough.

Maybe it's the idea of growing up.
Maybe that's it. Maybe it all comes down to just growing up.
And maybe ironically, I held onto the hope that I would forever be with my girls relishing everything that childhood brings.

But I cried today and I don't really know why.
Could it be all the times I messed up and felt completely alone?
Could it be never wanting my girls to feel alone themselves?
Could it be that now I will be alone with my husband, how it all began all those years ago?
I cried today.

Could it be I wonder where life will take you?
Could it be I wonder, truly wonder, if I did enough, taught you enough, held you enough, and if I filled you up with enough love?
Could it be because I always hope you will hear my voice whispering to you along the way?
Could it be because my wish is for all of your hopes and dreams to flourish and come true?
Could it be just being a mom?

Mama, maybe you are feeling this way too. I hold on believing I can't be the only mom feeling this push and pull of motherhood with the twists and turns spinning me around and around where I don't even know what is happening, but I'm allowing myself to feel it all without pushing it deep down into my gut.

I cried today and I cried a lot, and that is okay.

So for now, I'll embrace the tears that form as droplets roll down my cheek and get caught on my eyelashes just as I will always and forever embrace the flow of life and being a mom.

I cried today and what a gift it is to know maybe you're shedding a tear too right alongside of me, supporting me along my journey and new chapter in my life.

> *As a mother, I will never fully let go of all of the memories created and stored in a special place in my heart. Even though life is moving forward, and my children are grown, I will continue to stand off to the side, encouraging and supporting them with an unwavering amount of love.*

Reflection

Something I recently cried about. . .

Self-Love

Mama,
Can you do me a favor?

Take some time today to fill yourself up because no one else can do this for you.

Your cup needs to remain full so you can slowly release the gifts within you to those you love.

Don't wait for others, your kids, or your partner to make you happy.

You need to learn how to fill yourself up with joy.

Because here's the deal, one of the most important relationships we have is with ourselves.
If we don't love ourselves and offer ourselves self-care, how can we expect others to love us?

This is so hard for so many moms because we are giving out so much love to our kids and our family that we truly forget to take care of our own needs at times but this needs to stop.

So many of us are caught up in this trap, where we even think showering is self-love.

Self-Love

But Mama, showering is not self-love.

Brushing your teeth for two minutes is not self-love.

Sleeping is not self-love.

Those are necessary components to function as an adult woman.

Self-love goes beyond that. We need to incorporate this and build a connection with ourselves as much as possible and I want you to think about this way...

If we don't show self-love toward ourselves, how will our kids know how to love themselves?

We are their biggest role model.

They follow our lead, so therefore it's essential to learn how to incorporate self-love into our daily routine and model that as best as we can.

But you might be asking yourself where do I begin?

You may silently say to yourself, "I have been putting myself on hold for so long because I believed that self-care was selfish."

And the answer is this.

You need to nourish both your body and your soul and believe in the very depths of your soul that self-care is not selfish.

Self-care is necessary.

Self-care is what allows you to not spiral into the hole of feeling stuck, lost, bored, and uninspired.

Self-care is what keeps you grounded, rooted, and optimistic about life.

Mama, here's the thing about self-care...

Reflection is key! You must put time aside and put in the effort for self-reflection.

And you may ask yourself is it necessary and think to yourself,

> But I'm so busy, does self-care really matter? I don't have time for this. I'm busy at work. I'm busy with my kids. I wake up at five in the morning and I go to work and I have 200 people working under me. I have a crazy boss who's on my back like a hawk over me and helicoptering me and then I come home and I have to get my kids to their activities and I have to make dinner and I have to help with bedtime routine and I have to have conversation with my partner. Do I really need to do this?

The answer is yes !

We need to fill ourselves up in order to be the mom and the woman we are meant to be and the mom and the woman we want to be.

So get up and get going, Mama!
You've got this!

Finding myself is a form of self-care that goes beyond cups of coffee sitting in a quiet space alone, meditation, or slow walks on my favorite country road. Finding myself is accepting and loving myself for who I am today and allowing myself time to recalibrate and transform into the miraculous woman I am becoming.

Reflection

A few ways I incorporate self-love into my life. . .

This Is Motherhood

On the mantle in my family room is a painting I have stared at each day for the past 18 years. Some days I give it the full attention it deserves with utmost gratitude, and other days I offer a quick glance as I rush by focusing more on the demands of life. Many years ago I asked an acquaintance, who was a painter, to capture the simplicity of my life within her artwork so I would never forget the blessings of my pregnancies and children. I knew my words would never be able to capture fully the emotions inside of me surrounding my beautiful family, but the visual of a subdued painting would allow me to take pause and breathe new life into me each day as my eyes glanced over toward the wall.

Most would say the painting is simple at first sight. It's a bird's nest, intertwining branches and scraps that holds three white speckled eggs representing motherhood. My motherhood. My three pregnancies holding four healthy beautiful daughters.

There is such beauty to be found within the intricate parts of the nest created by the mother bird, just like my life. It's a compilation of my mistakes and hardships, challenges, and heartaches. It's my goals and aspirations, love, and compassion all woven together within each layer of the nest, our nest. It's creating a blanket of love with layers upon layers of devotion and time. It's grit and muck, beauty, and hard work capturing a life well lived, not perfect, but exactly what is right for my children. This is motherhood.

So each morning, as I walk down the stairs of our home, the painting that captures my life through a simple nest reminds me of the many layers of my life and raising my children. It's who I am as a woman and a mom, and I will never get tired of staring at the painting that greets me each day, reminding me to be who I need to be for my family. This is my motherhood.

Being a mother is embracing the simplicity of motherhood. It's within the simplicity that love is able to take over and guide us along our journey.

Reflection

A simple item that reminds me of my motherhood journey...

Little Pep Talks As I Walk

When I walk alone along the dusty gravel roads near my home, I talk aloud. I talk to the trees, the air, the sky. I talk to myself, allowing words to enter in to heal parts of myself I don't always understand or pay attention to and to talk through my motherhood journey.

I talk through all that I'm grateful for and the blessings of the simple things...
a hug from one of my daughters before bed, a short text just saying "Hi Mom," a coffee date when feeling disconnected to regroup ourselves and where we left off in the hustle and bustle of the morning before the day takes over, or a simple smile from one of my girls as she slowly exits the room.

But I also talk through what's troubling my heart...
my worries and fears, my self-doubt and the ever-imposing mom guilt I so often feel that keeps me awake at night, the words that should have been left unspoken, my quick and impulsive need to talk and offer advice right away, or the many ways I wonder how I can be a better mom.

You see, Mama, talking aloud may seem completely outlandish and a bit crazy to some, but to me, hearing the vibrations of my voice and the raw words escaping my lips grounds me. It brings me to a place of simplicity and a world where it's just me and my thoughts and a divine spirit of some sort that is larger than me. It allows me the freedom of words and to share what I'm often too scared or embarrassed to admit.

So I continue to walk and I talk and as I wander I continue to ponder all of the emotions that take over this heart of mine. A heart that never knew how many emotions were hidden inside of this miraculous body and spirit until I became a mom.

And as I continue my journey of being a mom, I foresee that I will keep talking aloud, no matter where my path leads, to become the mom and woman I hope to one day be.

> *Motherhood is a whirlwind filled with love, overwhelm, compassion, and pure exhaustion. Motherhood is all of this and more but as moms, we keep showing up day and day to love our children with all our heart can offer.*

Reflection

Words I silently speak to my heart. . .

Now I Get It

I don't know why I always feel I need to straighten up the house before I leave, but today was no exception. Mama, do you ever do this?

Why do I need to put on one more load of laundry before running out of the door, and why do I worry every time I leave if I left the candle on to then find myself driving back through the neighborhood and up the driveway to realize that no, I didn't leave the candle on, but I have zero recollection of blowing the candle out since I was sidetracked by an email reminding me to do something. But now, 15 minutes later and the minutes add up and then there you go, I'm late once again.

Why do I feel when I ask my kids to do something it never gets done so now as they all hop in the car waiting for me, with keys in hand, I am completing the task before pulling out of the garage. But once again I arrive at my destination exhausted.

Mama, we need to lift each other up in these moments of overwhelm.
We need to offer support and validation and not judge, ridicule, or criticize one another if we are late and barely make it on time. We need to hold each other's hands and let one another know we are not alone.

Now I Get It

We need to pull one another up from out of the trenches when we are lost in the muck.
We need to wrap one another in an embrace and exhale.

So many of us are simply struggling to just hold on, and we need another mom to love us because the hard truth is we can't do it all, and that's okay, Mama.

So many of us feel a loss within ourselves and fall into the vicious cycle of doing and going and going and doing while feeling guilty if something isn't complete, and that's exactly why we are the last one in the car and faithfully running late.

And this, Mama, is the cycle of motherhood.
It's a cycle of generations who feel guilty, not enough, and are trapped feeling we cannot be our authentic selves if it shows anything less than perfection.

As this pattern continues for me even with teens, I've been thinking maybe moms are late because we aren't always asking for the help we need, but more importantly we often aren't getting the support and help from our partners. . .so we're late.

Maybe we're late because we're picking up the pillows and folding the blankets that have been a mess on the couch and we have asked countless times for our teen to straighten up.

Maybe we're making sure the toilets are flushed and every light in the house is off and the flat iron has been turned off even though we've checked it ten times.

Or maybe we're late because we are taking on too much and it's a lot for one person to carry this load each day.

So Mama, let's promise each other this. . .we will not judge one another whether we are two minutes late or a half hour late, and rather we will understand and silently give a glance knowing and understanding exactly why, with no other explanation needed. But most importantly maybe we can begin to offer a helping hand to help ease the load of motherhood and lift one another up because one day we may need the support too. We never know what is going on in someone's world, or the weight they carry, so let's give grace to ourselves and one another.

> *Today I am letting go of the weight that is holding me back and suffocating me at times. Today I am releasing my mom guilt and giving myself the grace I deserve. Today I am wrapping myself up in love and recognizing I can't do it all.*
> *Today I am allowing myself to say aloud I am not meant to do it all.*

Reflection

One thing that's holding me back. . .

It's a Marathon, Not a Sprint

Motherhood is a marathon, not a sprint.
It's slow and steady.
It's setting a pace and not impulsively moving forward.
It's taking a breath, pausing, and being mindful that this is a slow journey, not one moment in time.

Our motherhood journey is filled with moments that we often want to race through when filled with disarray and complete overwhelm.
It's moments where messiness takes over, we wish we could erase today, or at the very least fast-forward to tomorrow.
It's times that bring us to our knees where we wish we could put life on pause but the truth is we can't.

Motherhood is a marathon, not a sprint.

This marathon of motherhood requires nourishing our bodies, our souls, and our hearts.

Motherhood requires us to put one foot in front of the other, even when we are filled with fatigue and fight to the very end to remain balanced.

Motherhood requires us to find the right pace to carry us through the lengthy days, while filling our bodies up with what we need, and fueling ourselves to move forward to what's ahead.

Motherhood requires us to care for ourselves, love ourselves, and take notice of our own needs because if we don't, we will fall to the ground with exhaustion.
But most of all, motherhood requires us to slow down.

Motherhood is a marathon, not a sprint.

Mama, it's not a race to see who gets to the finish line first because there is no finish line in life.
It's not a time to break a personal record because being a mom is about creating our own time frame as we navigate this journey.
And it's not a time to win any prizes or fancy awards or to receive any trophies or accolades.

Motherhood is simply a marathon of loving, nurturing, and nourishing.

It's moments we can't rush, for it has to be tended to no differently than our garden or training our body for a race.

We have to tend to the parts that are in the weakest condition.
We need to hold close our greatest fears knowing those moments of weakness move us forward with confidence.
And we need to believe that in due time we will get to the other side.

Mama, motherhood is a marathon, not a sprint.
Keep this close to your heart.

Slow down, soak it all in, and recognize that beauty is found within the most ordinary moments. These are the moments our hearts will recall with laughter and joy will enter our souls. These are the moments creating a lifetime of memories to hold onto forever.

Reflection

A way I'm slowing down on my motherhood journey. . .

I'm Worthy Too

As my college daughter and I sat in the airport terminal waiting to board two different flights, after a long weekend spent together, she leaned over and gently said, "Mom you need to believe in yourself the way that you believe in me. You need to believe the same way that you have taught me and my sisters to believe in ourselves. You need to gain your confidence back, and you need to be secure again. You need to be that person because that is who you taught us to be."

It's not that often I find myself speechless but in this moment, boarding pass and carry on in hand, I lost words as my breath was sucked out of me.
I felt caught because she saw right into the deepest parts of me as the announcement that my flight was boarding echoed through the terminal.
With a tearful goodbye and a lump in my throat holding my breath, I slowly embarked down the ramp headed toward the gate, to catch my flight home. I finally caught my breath as the cool air rushed through the corridor and my daughter's words kept echoing in my mind. She was right. My girl was spot on and saw right through me. In recent years I let go of the confidence I used to exude, and she gently reminded me this is not who I am.

I'm Worthy Too

Is it from the changing body that stares at me each time I cross paths with my mirror?

Is it being at a crossroads entering a new phase of motherhood and figuring out who I am while entering empty nesting?

Or maybe it's the new empty nesting woman taking over my soul as I try to find myself once again?

I'm not sure, but you know what, Mama, she's right.

I'm not the same confident woman who once stood before her and she misses the old me.
I miss the old me.

As a mom, I take great pride as I boost my kids up and cheer them on when they need to be fueled with endless amounts of encouragement to keep going, and I continue to endlessly support them when their self-esteem plummets.
It doesn't matter if it's about friendships, academics, body image, relationships, extra-curricular activities, or self-love. I am always encouraging and supporting while reminding them that they have so much to offer the world.

So as my plane began to take flight and I soared above the tree line and billowing clouds, I felt tears escaping from my eyes and gently falling soft upon my cheek.

I couldn't help but ruminate on this one thought...
If I can offer words of affirmation and encouraging words that build confidence for my college kids, why do I have such a hard time doing it for myself? Why can't I give myself the same self-love?

I may not have found the answer within the clouds that late Sunday afternoon, but I did find hope in my daughter's words reminding me that I am worthy of reuniting with the confident woman I once was.

We all struggle with self-doubt and feeling not enough. Offer yourself grace today to go back to the woman you once were, embrace the woman you are becoming, and allow yourself to be the authentic woman you are.
You are loved.

Reflection

A few ways I remind myself I am worthy. . .

Here's to You, Mama

Here's to the mama running on empty.
The mama overwhelmed yet filled with joy.
The mama struggling to find her way some days yet still holds her family close.

Here's to the mama holding on tight yet still trying to find her way to hang in there.
She is filled with hope and optimism, grace and gratitude.
Here's to you, Mama.
You are doing a wonderful job, and I felt like you needed to hear that today.
You are doing an amazing job.

I am a good mom even on the days I don't perceive this to be true. I need to remind myself that I am doing my best each day and that is more than enough.

Reflection

A few things I'm doing right now as a mom that I'm proud of...

A Mother's Hope

I hope I'm the first person my daughter thinks to call when she's bored or wants to speak freely about what's on her heart.

I hope our connection can surpass the end of time and continue to connect us for a lifetime.

I yearn for a relationship that's overflowing with quality time together, showing up for one another, and loving each other through the highs and lows.

I yearn to always be her safe haven and continuously encourage her even as battles take over her heart.

I hope our laughter washes away any venomous words that seep out of our mouths and come pouring out of our hearts.

I hope I always feel a gentle yet beautiful tug at my heart as her grace enters the room and fills my soul with gratitude.

I yearn to know that the times I never gave up on her, on me, on us, allow for a light to shine revealing the bigger picture of who we are together.

I yearn to know her trials and tribulations, fulfilled dreams, and breathtaking opportunities before her.

A Mother's Hope

I hope I allow her to feel her feelings and chase after her dreams, not mine, while understanding who she is along her intimate journey of life.
I hope my greatest blessing in life will always yearn to pick up the phone to call her mama.

I yearn to know her to the depths of her soul.

I hope...

My wish is for my kids to know I always have their back.
I want them to one day look back and know I loved them fiercely.

Reflection

A few things I hope for in my relationship with my child/children...

Would You Know?

As you read this letter, I encourage you to take a few moments to reflect on what you would want your kids to know about you, not just as their mom, but as the woman raising them.

Dear Daughter,

If my soul left this earth tomorrow...

Would you know my heart skips a beat when I see a beautiful hue of pink emerge in the late spring, bringing life to the hydrangeas surrounding my yard and how the salty ocean air embraces a deep part of me nothing else can touch?

Or how when I gaze out at the horizon, watching pelicans soar along the top layer of the sea, I feel both joyful and sad?

Are you aware the sea brings back old memories yet soothes an ache in my heart bringing about happiness like a long lost friend, and as my teeth bite down on a crisp, yet soft, Rice Krispies treat, I'm filled with childhood enthusiasm?

Would You Know?

Or how I believe arguments aren't just fighting but rather a way to connect more, learn more, and love more?

Would you know I also love to run? I yearn to run off stress, run off regrets, run off frustration, run off thoughts I can't share or thoughts I share too much, and run off the energy built up inside of me.

Or that behind my often stoic face I'm a woman with a thousand emotions, about to burst, yet holding back and how I hate rainbow sherbet but becoming a mother changed every cell in my body?

Are you aware my stomach speaks all of the words I suppress and my heart has healed many times through words which are the balm to my soul just as laughter makes my heart happy?

Or how much I adore people who speak transparently and show their authentic self?

Would you know sitting in silence brings me peace and renewal and my family means everything to me?

Or that keeping women safe is close to my heart? Everyone should feel loved and be able to be who they are and not controlled.

Are you aware that I don't like musicals and my soul was born to dance while my children and their wild spirits set me free and inspire me to dream?

Or how old friends touch a part of my soul so very few are allowed to enter?

Would you know romance makes me giddy and taking drives in the open air with the wind blowing through my hair makes me feel alive and how each night, as I close my eyes, I wonder how I can be better tomorrow?

Or how a gentle walk fills my soul and allows a divine spirit to seep inside and open me up to new thoughts?

Are you aware your laughter takes my pain away and I love you more than words can ever say?

Would you know...

It is important for motherhood to be filled with moments of solitude and time for deep reflection. The beauty of this time is that it's within these quiet moments you learn about yourself while the silence surrounding you embraces you in love. It's within the silence we learn who we truly are and begin to let that light shine out into the world and into our children's hearts.

Reflection

A few things I want my child/children to know more deeply about me...

I hope my children look back one day and know that even though I made many mistakes along the way, I always had their back loving and guiding them. I may not have always done the right thing but one thing never wavered. I always offered all of the love I had and then some more.

PART

Raising Teens

I may not be a perfect mom,
but I promise you this…
You will always be my everything.

Introduction to Raising Teens

At one point a few years ago, all four of my girls were in high school at the same time. I felt torn in a multitude of directions and some days felt emotionally dried up. During this time, though, I learned two key components about raising teens. One is that laughter could cure most of the things that were pressing on their hearts, and the second is that through the challenges they faced, as long as they felt an overflowing amount of love, they would be okay.

Through the teen years, love prevailed even on the most difficult of days.
Love got us through the challenging times and the times of deep hurt.
Love carried us through the trials of being a teen with all of the emotional baggage that too often teens drag around behind them and love kept us connected even at times where we felt disconnected.

No matter how tired or exhausted I was, what drama was taking place, or how deeply drained I felt from feeling like I wasn't doing a good enough job as their mom, I continued to love. Because you see, Mama, the truth is, *mom's love hard and then they love some more*. It's what moms do and it's what we will continue to do until our very last breath.

But Mama, let me clarify, as much as I loved hard, I also deeply struggled through *many* moments during the teenage years. Some days I found myself going on a long drive in my car, feeling completely overwhelmed while searching desperately for some emotional relief. I was worn out, anxious, and pushed to a breaking point. I had to accept that taking a respite in the comfort of my car was okay and it was an outlet for me to escape, for a short time, from the emotional demands of motherhood. Some days I drove around the neighborhood, other days it was the back country roads staring at the dirt road ahead and the beauty of the horses surrounding me that offered me grace, and sometimes it was a quick trip to the drive through of McDonald's for a fountain Diet Coke.

The car was a place for me to gather my thoughts and regroup myself so I could be the mom I wanted to be. The moments in my car though weren't something to be ashamed of. This time alone, surrounded by the quiet comfort of a small space, gave me great clarity. Sometimes I simply needed to gather my composure, take a few deep breaths, and quickly move forward in order to be the mom I needed to be for my girls. This time alone gave me the opportunity to reflect on situations that took me off guard and ease my mind on those days when the chaos became too much to handle.

I took this time to regroup, refocus, and make every attempt to move forward in a positive and productive way. I made space for myself while recognizing that this motherhood gig isn't always easy. Maybe every now and then you find yourself making a mad dash to the car or your safe space also, or maybe you retreat and binge watch the latest series, and Mama, I want you to know that is more than okay.

As I traveled my motherhood journey raising teens, I realized something else. No matter what was going on in my girls' world at the time, they all needed one thing…love. They needed to feel loved and be loved.

So on the days I was faced with silly arguments over hair ties, jean shorts, or whose socks were whose, my love needed to be present.

On the days it felt like the entire house was silently ignoring one another for no reason at all, my love needed to be present.

On the days big issues came up causing my teen and I to raise our voices over curfews, boundaries, and the looming thought of letting go while allowing more independence, my love needed to be present.

And on the days I was withering away, feeling worn out, overwhelmed, and down right exhausted, my love still needed to be present.
Mama, if you are entering the teenage years or you are in the thick of it right now, just know this time doesn't last forever. It's a moment, a little snippet, that's all. A moment in time filled with an enormous amount of emotions for both you and your teen, but just one moment along your motherhood journey.

The mood swings, eye rolls, and challenging behavior is all temporary, if it's even present at all, so please trust me on this. It's important though to remember that within all of the chaos entering this new chapter, there is also a breathtaking space where we can make room to see the beauty within our teens and who they are as their authentic selves. This right here is the gift our teens offer to us and the world around us. The gift of witnessing the emotional growth of the amazing person standing before us.

So Mama, just remember, whether you have blissful days or days filled with hiccups and hardships, you are not alone. We have all have had those days when we feel the weight of the world on our shoulders and it's hard to even take a breath. But remember, I am here cheering for you, supporting you, and encouraging you along this phase of your motherhood journey especially during those moments you are in your car taking the deep breaths you need in order to keep moving forward. You've got this!

What does it mean to be a mother?

It's a rollercoaster of emotions defining a life filled with intense love and a desire to protect your child no matter how old they may be.

Holding On While Shifting

Motherhood is filled with many shifts and I'm feeling one big time right now.

I'm trying to not get caught up in my feelings too much since I'm filled with a lot of disappointment and sadness, but some days it's just hard to not go down that path.
My world feels like I'm on a Scrambler ride at the carnival and I'm waiting for it to stop, but it keeps going faster and faster, shifting directions, and I can't get off the ride as hard as I try. My world feels rocked right now because I have entered the part of my journey where I feel my daughter slipping away.

One day we were side-by-side doing everything together and then the next morning – BOOM! – a cosmic shift took place shaking things up. We went from spending all of our time together running errands, baking cookies, watching movies snuggled up on the couch, and chatting it up in the kitchen to silence, complete and utter silence. In what seemed like a moment, life shifted, and I'm not really liking it if I'm being honest.

No longer is my girl right by my side and Mama, it tugs at my heart. This subtle shift feels like my connection to my girl is crashing down and crumbling around me, and I wonder if you ever feel this way some days.

Holding On While Shifting

I feel overwhelmed by the new grunts and groans when I ask a simple question and I miss our hugs as she enters a room. My breath even seems to annoy her and let's not even discuss when I chew.
Will it be like this forever?
Will she come back around?
What can I do to make this process easier on my heart?

There are days I simply miss hugging my daughter. I miss the moments where she is frantically rushing out of the house, water bottle in hand as I try to sneak in one hug before the school day begins. On other days I miss the moments sitting on the couch, as the fireplace crackles, arm and arm laughing over a story she just told me. But some days I just miss her even though we live under the same roof.

Mama, you know what I have realized though during the many sleepless nights I lay awake retracing this shift over and over again in my mind? This is all normal.
It may not seem normal, and I may hate every moment of it but it's a natural progression for our kids to pull away and as moms, we need to give them this space to grow. I keep thinking that this slight shift is what will eventually bridge the gap between us in the near future and that by allowing the time and space to grow my daughter will come back around eventually.

So rather than allowing this time of transition and shifting to take over my mama heart with sadness, I'm keeping an eye on the future and to find the connections that will reunite us once again. Because Mama, it's in the reconnection where we learn, heal, and grow alongside one another. So for now, I will patiently wait for another shift to eventually take place allowing room for more growth.

Will I be okay during these shifts? Yes!
Will I need the support of my partner and friends and some extra TLC? Maybe.
Will I continue to hope and pray that a deeper relationship and connection forms in the future? Absolutely!

So Mama, if you are in a place of shifting, hold tight. The day will come where life aligns once again and our hearts can settle down peacefully knowing all is right in the world.

One of the hardest parts of motherhood is recognizing that within each new season of parenting you and your child will both grow and change, always needing to adapt to each new season for what it is and who you are both becoming.

Reflection

A shift that is taking place in my life. . .

Falling Short, Maybe Not

Do you ever feel like you're falling short?
That even on your very best day it's not enough?
This feeling has been taking over my heart a lot lately.
I know I'm trying my best, but it feels like I can never meet the needs of everyone.
But the more I think about this it's not my teens making me feel this way, it's me.

They aren't complaining about what I made for dinner or that I forgot to sign them up on the parent portal for something for school.
They aren't annoyed that I asked them the same question over and over again even though they answered me two days ago and I just forgot.
They are content. They love and accept me for me.

So why do I place these unnecessary demands on myself when no one else is?
Why do I let guilt take over my soul and suffocate me?
Why do I feel like I'm drowning in a lost world and I can't climb my way out of it?

And then it hits me...

It's because we live in a world where motherhood is supposed to look a certain way, yet in reality it doesn't.
So when it doesn't fit the mold we take a pause and notice every missing detail and flaw.
And then down the rabbit hole we go.

So today, I'm taking a pause and noticing the good that I do.
Because you see, Mama, if I keep going through the nonsense of what I'm supposed to be like, based on unrealistic expectations society has placed on me, what am I teaching my teens?
That they too need to be the teen society represents them as?
A teen who is sassy and snotty, obnoxious and knows it all, disrespectful and distant?
My teens have broken barriers. They haven't fallen into this trap, so why do I?
They are my role model for moving forward, not allowing false parameters or pretenses to be placed on them or on me.

Remember the older women in the grocery store calling out, "Just wait until the teen years! Good luck!"
Well, let me tell you a secret.
I love the teen years. It's a time filled with electricity and excitement, compassion, and the need to still want to be coddled while they are also spreading their wings. They relish in the delight of the little moments while setting goals for the future and with wide eyes make every attempt to attain these goals.

Our teens are filled with a magic inside of them.
It's the magic of seeing the world through a different lens while breaking cycles and creating new paths.

Our teens are filled with a desire that encourages and inspires others to not let false expectations define them.

Our teens are filled with a magic that electrifies all that is to come in the future and they give me hope.

So today, I'm going to believe this truth my teens have placed within my heart and move forward knowing I'm not falling short on my motherhood journey yet rather I'm growing and learning alongside them and that is always enough.

The truth about raising teens that most people don't talk about is how incredible they can be. Our teens have the ability to fill up our lives with an intense energy and spirit that makes us laugh until we cry. They know exactly how to take this stressed out mama and turn her day around. Growing up beside my teen and evolving together, side by side, has been one of life's greatest blessings bestowed upon me.

Reflection

A way I have grown along my journey while raising a teen...

The Open Road

There was a time not too long ago where my daughter and I kept butting heads. We couldn't see eye to eye, and I was fearful of what was to become of us and the adult relationship I had always envisioned.

We both knew something had to change, but we weren't quite sure how to accomplish this. I couldn't fathom how to fix this or for the life of me why we were going down this path. She was an amazing kid. She was loving toward others, a great student, kept her room clean (which is half the battle for moms raising teens), and wonderful to be around, but something was missing for us and our connection.

I would ask myself as I lay in bed at night, was I pushing her on things that didn't matter?
Was I just an annoying mom?
Is it just hormones surging through and taking its course as she enters the teen years?

I kept wondering if any other moms raising teenage daughters felt this same way.

One morning I remember sitting down with her and shared with her that we were too important to give up on and reminded her of my commitment to this relationship and how I would never give up on us. She was too important to me. We were to important to me. And in this moment, I realized something. We were more alike than we admitted, and too often this was what was getting in the way.

Mama, I felt overwhelmed and drained at times, but I also made a commitment to myself for some self-improvement. I put in effort daily to spend time reflecting on how to reconnect with myself and my daughter. I began daily meditation for clarity and patience, taking long walks outside, and journaling what was troubling me as well as what I was grateful for. This was a slow immersion, but something that had to be done. I needed to care for myself in order to care for and give to my daughter what she needed during these pressing and stressful teenage years.

But here's the thing that I believe changed everything...
I started to ask my daughter to come with me on long walks. The first few times I asked she told me how she hates walking and said no. Then one morning as I was about to head out the door, she appeared in her workout clothes and sneakers ready to join me. Can you say my mama heart skipped a beat? You bet it did!

And so it began...
My daughter and I walking side-by-side talking, laughing, and sharing our hearts. The gravel country roads became a balm to soothe our hearts and a Band-Aid to the wounds that were hurting us. The open road allowed honesty to seep out and a connection to develop after years of painfully admitting we were both hurting.

Let me clarify though; our relationship isn't always perfect, nor will it ever be, because let's be honest, real perfection doesn't exist.

And by no means should we ever place that expectation on ourselves or our teen, but we can have a relationship where we laugh, share the truth, and enjoy being near one another.

We hurt and we forgive.
We love and learn from each other.
And now, guess what? She lives miles away from home, attending college, but she calls me on her walks to and from class and what a blessing it is to remain connected. These calls each day I hold close to my heart in a very special place.

Mama, the open road is truly what healed our hearts and opened us up to a world of connection because we found a way that worked for us. Maybe you can find something that works for you too if you are also struggling during this part of your journey. Maybe you and your teen can go outside and shoot some baskets, or go on a drive, spend time chatting on the chairlift during a day of skiing, or even just find time sitting on the couch together watching a show. It's about doing what works for you and what will also heal your hearts.

If you are feeling disconnected and deep pain and sadness, don't give up, Mama!
There is always a new day tomorrow offering a clean slate to let go of the past, allow forgiveness to enter in, and put one foot in front of the other to continue on the path of opening up the door to the relationship that is ahead of you.
Raising a teen is often a journey about healing and renewal.

Mama, I know you have the tools to transform your connection. Trust me, if I can do it, you can too!

Just as the tide ebbs and flows so does the connection between mother and child.
They are both learning and evolving, growing and maturing alongside of one another. And just as the tide greets the shore each day, so does a mother as she greets her child with unwavering open arms.

Reflection

One way I can attempt to improve my connection with my teen...

Tearful Smile

With a tearful smile, I fondly recall your little hand swirling around in the magenta paint, proud as can be, to stamp your mark on the crisp white paper.

I find the past few days memories have been popping up, and as the movie reel of life keeps rolling, a tearful smile takes over my heart.

As a mom, sometimes I'm on my knees wishing for the day to rapidly fast-forward or to get through a certain phase, but other days I'm grasping frantically for the rewind button to stop time and soak it all in.

I can't stop life from happening and growing around me.
I can't stop my children from growing up.

But I can embrace it and allow myself to feel it.

Through a tearful smile memories keep taking over my heart.

As I reflect, nostalgia takes over as I see you dancing around the kitchen in your cookie man shirt and a "pull-pup" on your head.

Tearful Smile

As I reflect, pride takes over, at the memory of how you once struggled through the torturous reading comprehension activities but still remained confident.

As I reflect, joy embraces me, at the memory of how you persevered through middle school and navigated the days that overflowed with insecurities and those awkward moments of self-doubt.

As I reflect, strength surrounds me and reminds me of the day you didn't make the school team but asked, that same day, to practice to improve your game.

As I reflect, happiness consumes my heart, as I remember how you received accolades of praise from teachers about your kind heart and desire to help others.

My tearful smile, sweet child, is deep rooted in love.

My tearful smile is pure amazement at how you tackle challenges with grace.

My tearful smile reflects the pride I feel for who you are and for all you are bound to become.

So as I gently wipe away my tears of joy, I believe for a moment, the movie reel has paused...

I can still feel your five-year-old hand, entwined in mine, swinging through the air.

But as the movie reel keeps playing, what I truly feel is the warmth of a woman, holding my hand, who reflects inner strength, confidence, and copious amounts of love.

I don't need the movie reel to pause. . .

I simply need to live in the moment, holding your hand.

> *The essence of being a mother is looking at your children and thinking, "My greatest accomplishment in life is standing right in front of me."*

Reflection

A way I'm living in the moment with my teen. . .

If Only I Knew

If I knew the two of us would one day end up in this place of friendship, maybe I would not have worried as much.
If I knew the space I envisioned and dreamed for us would come true, maybe it wouldn't have been necessary to sit on my prayers and continue to hope as we navigated the early teen years.
If I knew, maybe those moments of pure anxiety would have been smoothed over with peace, knowing in due time my girl and I would be giggling over dinner, dancing the night away belting out our of favorite songs with a giddiness about our twining hats, and my heart would have felt lighter.
If I knew, maybe those sleepless nights would have been less and holding on to what we had in that very moment would have been a calm reassurance to soothe my soul.
If I knew our worlds would one day mesh and not feel so distant and torn apart, then maybe all of those tears I shed would have been met with a smile.

So now, as I glance over at my girl, I know with deep conviction we have reached our destination.
A beautiful destination filled with laughter, hugs, conversations filled with depth, secrets, and a space where as mother and daughter we are our true selves.
And I am washed over with peace.

If I knew we would eventually get to this place, maybe my heart wouldn't have been so weary at times, but to be honest, I wouldn't have changed a thing about the journey we traveled together to get to our divine destination of a lifelong friendship.
If only I knew.

> *Learning to laugh through the heartache is the very best medicine we can ever offer to ourselves as mothers. Every season will have its struggles and hardships but it's how we reach into our souls, dig deep, and emerge from it that makes all the difference.*

Reflection

Something I would have done differently if only I knew. . .

Our Teens Need Us

Our teens need us even when it doesn't seem that way.

They need us when they're lashing out and we feel that we are the last person on earth they want to be near. They need us through the grunts, eye rolls, and slammed doors.

They need us when they are smiling and thriving about life and when they are mourning in misery and everything is our fault.

They need us when we don't say anything right, the way we breathe annoys them, or God forbid we sneeze.

They need us when they look to us for guidance, support, and sharing their most vulnerable selves.

They need us when they seem mature, have it all together, happiness abounds, and also when sadness takes over their hearts, anxiety creeps in, and they simply can't explain the mix of emotions they are encountering.

They need us to encourage them, reminding them of their strengths when they're on top of the world and when everything is falling to pieces.

Our teens need us.

They need us for a quick chat in the kitchen, munching on chips, and during the late hours of the night as they sit in the dark pouring their hearts out as our eyes are filled with fatigue yet love encapsulates our hearts.

They need us when they are feeling overwhelmed and stressed, torn in a multitude of directions, and can barely add one more thing to their plate and also when the day is like a light breeze, floating in with ease as the day takes over, filling their souls with joy.

They need us when they are on a clear path filled with visions and goals, and they need us when they don't know where their path leads, where their journey will take them, or how they will find their way navigating the crazy world that awaits them.

They need us when they have it all planned out, perfectly aligned, and they need us when life is overwhelming and the idea of a plan causes anxiety to creep in and rear its dark side.

They need us especially when it's hard for them to show love.

They need us through lost friendships and broken hearts as they attempt to mend their souls and when they are loving wildly and feel deeply rooted and connected.

Our teens need us.

They need us to love them for who they are, the imperfectly perfect human that they are becoming even if they are not following the path we envisioned for them.

They need us to show them who we truly are, without holding back, while offering up the brutal truth that sometimes life is hard but there is always hope in the days ahead.

They need us to love them fiercely forever and always.

Our teens need us.

> *As I gaze at my teen I am silently cheering for my younger self as well.*
> *I'm filling her up with the confidence she needs to take on the world, not fall into the comparison trap, and love herself for who she is. These silent cheers then allow me, as a mom, to offer my teen the motivation and love I needed back then and the desire for her to keep on going.*

Reflection

A few ways my teen needs me and how I can best support them through the process of growing up...

24/7

As she tiptoed in the room I heard, "Mom, can we talk?"
I opened my eyes, a bit groggy and out of it, and saw the clock announcing it was 2 a.m. As most mama hearts would do, I immediately sat up wondering, with a bit of fright, if everything was okay. To my relief there was no emergency, everyone was breathing, a fire wasn't barreling its way through the house, and she was safe and sound wrapped up in a cozy blanket with monkey pillow in hand standing next to my bed.

I moved over to make space for her but quietly my mind began to wander and worry.
Is she okay?
What's going on?
Did I miss seeing something important?
Do I need to call in reinforcements?

As she sat next to me, in the darkness of the night, with a dim light entering the room, I realized something magical was taking place. My girl came to me with her deepest worries and secrets simply needing a listening ear, a heart that would understand her, and a hug to carry her through the night.

Overall, she was okay. She just had some pressing thoughts taking over causing some anxiety and worry. But you see Mama, the magic for me within this moment is that she knew she could come to me no matter what time it was. She knew after years of me openly reminding her that I was available day or night and I would be there. She knew she could trust me to listen with a full heart and offer her the validation she needed to hear and the words of comfort her heart needed to absorb and digest.

But, Mama, sometimes these conversations don't go as planned as we know all too well. Sometimes as moms we need to be prepared to hear news that we either weren't expecting or we don't always want to hear. And sometimes we have to dig deep, really deep, to provide the love and comfort our teen needs even when we disagree with them, or feel torn apart.

But we have to remember this...
We are their support.
We are their lifeline and we are the boat that can carry them to shore.

My mama heart may have been completely fatigued as the hours of the night rolled by that evening, but my heart was also full knowing the trust that had been fostered since childhood came knocking on my door at 2 a.m. and what a gift that is to treasure.

A mother is a child's safe haven and comfort.
A mother is love.

Reflection

A way I can show my teen I am there for them 24/7...

Patiently Waiting

My daughter is struggling with something pressing on her heart, and there is absolutely nothing I can do about it to take her pain away. It's a struggle only she can resolve and move forward from. It's not my place to intervene, so I gently need to make sure that I'm not crossing any boundaries, but to be honest, Mama, all I want to do is rescue her.

I want to take it all on and make the pain go away just as her bunny did so many nights as a little girl.
I want to smooth it all out for her so she doesn't have to go through the long process of healing, but I can't.

I feel helpless but this space is where I need to remain.
I need to stay in this space and wait patiently for her to come to me to work through this if she chooses to want my help.
But the tricky part is she needs to come to me.
I can't infringe on her life, and I can't take over.
She is a young adult and in the position where she can do this alone, but oh my heart, I wish I could speed this process up for her.
She knows I'm always available to talk through things, and she knows I will walk this part of her journey by her side.

But, Mama, it's her choice now if she chooses to get me involved or not and all my heart can do is sit on the sidelines waiting.

Patiently Waiting

I know so many other mamas are dealing with moments in their life like this too, for so many different reasons and scenarios, so let's stay strong waiting patiently together for the day our teen reaches out their hand inviting us into their world and the many things that are pressing on their heart as they navigate this time in life.

> *Being a mom to a teen is often waiting in the space between as they figure out their own path and course of life. It's not about what we have envisioned for our teen but rather allowing them the time and space to figure it out on their own.*

Reflection...

Waiting is hard. A few things I'm waiting on with my teen...

A Mother's Warmth

As the gray wool wraps around my fingers attempting to weave together each row, I'm reminded of the lifetime of memories my daughter and I have woven together. From the first moment she was delicately placed in my arms our intricate dance of weaving a life together began. It's a love with no end, no bounds, and a love that reaches in deep and takes the breath right out of my lungs. It's the love of a mother.

So as I sit on the floor, legs crossed and snow falling outside as a massive amount of gray wool surrounds me, I am quickly reminded of the fabric of our being. Just as the wool has some parts that are subtle and smooth while other areas are coarse, lacking some softness and hard to weave together effortlessly, so is motherhood and raising children.

But it's the weaving together of both that creates the beauty within the blanket and the magic of the two parts woven together to create a mother.

It's the brutal days filled with emotions you didn't know existed before becoming a mother and moments of pure elation on the days your motherhood journey is going right as planned. It's the push and pull. The known and the unknown. The weaving in and out that once complete creates a masterpiece waiting to be admired.

So as I continue to weave together parts of our life, the obstacles and struggles, times of utter joy and gratefulness, I realize something, I wouldn't change a thing. Because it's within the ying and the yang of motherhood I have learned the most. It's within the moments of frustration and times of struggle that challenge me to do better and be better. It's within the miscounted rows, where I lost my way, that I have learned life lessons to move forward.

Life isn't linear.
Motherhood isn't simple.
We are human.
We ebb and flow while creating space between the ins and outs.
The pattern created will never be perfect.
It's the complicated pattern of memories woven to last a lifetime as mother and child.

As my daughter holds the blanket woven by my hands may she one day be reminded of my love emanating from the warmth of the blanket where our hearts were woven together binding us for a lifetime, even with large holes within missing rows.

Watching your first born grow up hits different.
They are the ones that taught you how to be a mama.
They are the ones that changed your life.

Reflection

A way my child will always feel my warmth...

Catch Me

As she steadies herself on the rock and takes the leap, flying through the air as if she has the courage of Super Woman, she is filled with exhilaration and delight. Her spirit lifts, confidence beams, and as she lands in my arms, she knows she is safe.
And she does this again and again knowing my presence will always be a constant.

I am her safe place.

She knows I will always catch her and wrap her in love and support.

Some days, I miss hearing her sweet voice call out, "Mama, catch me!"
But then I take pause and realize even though she is almost an adult, embarking on flying from the nest, I'm still here catching her.

Maybe she's not jumping into my arms anymore but catching her now has a new twist.
Mama, maybe your motherhood role is shifting with some new twists also that you are adjusting to and figuring out along the way.

But I know one thing to be true, I will continue to catch her when she needs validation as she struggles with a decision.

I will continue to catch her when she needs a friend to lean on and no one is around.
I will continue to catch her to lift her up and keep her moving forward, guiding her along the way.
I will catch her as she sinks down into a hole filled with insecurities.
I will catch her as she seeks out love but feels discouraged.
I will catch her as she attempts to make sense of this massive world we live in.
I will catch her when she simply needs to feel my touch.

Catching my precious girl may have moved from the rock in the yard she once stood on as she waited patiently for the school bus to now the emotional needs of an adult embarking on a new journey, but one thing will always remain. . .

I will always be here to catch her.

> *No matter how old my kids are I will always encourage and support them throughout their lifetime. It's who I am.*
> *I AM A MOM!*

Reflection

A way I will continue to catch my child even when they're grown. . .

Side-by-Side

All I can do some days is walk with my teen through their disappointment, their heartache, break-ups, and their letdowns. It's a part of life, but it's also a part that tugs at this mama's heartstrings.

You see, Mama, I have spent my entire motherhood journey protecting my child's heart, watching out for them, being a shield when things got too close that were going to stab at them, speaking up for them when they didn't have the words to utter, cheering for them when they were down in the trenches and didn't know where to go, hauling them up, lifting them up, and supporting them throughout every twist and turn. I bet you have done this too on your journey.

But as my teens are getting older, I find it's getting harder and harder. As the older moms in Target once told me as a young mom with four girls under four, "bigger kids, bigger problems." Oh my heart, they weren't wrong. Gone are the days where Animal Crackers made everything right and my hugs and kisses cured all heartache. Can we just go back there for one moment in time though? My heart may need a break.

Now, as budding teens, it's not uncommon for disappointments to come at them left and right, surprising them and taking their breath away even when they are feeling on top of the world, and often taking away the confidence they once held so tight. I find many nights I am also left feeling defenseless, breathless, and not sure how to help.

Whether it's not getting on the sports team they wished, it's getting rejected from their first choice college or feeling the heartache of young love lost.
Or maybe it's being blatantly ignored by those they thought were friends and feeling that no matter how hard they try things just aren't going as planned.

I can't help but ask myself, how do I protect their heart, but also, selfishly, how do I protect my own heart?

How do I make sure that I have the balance to not step on their toes and intrude in their personal life, yet walk with them through their journey?
How do I support them while not giving too much advice or too many opinions? There's a fine line that I am so scared to cross because if I cross it there is a chance that I will lose them. But all I want to do is guide them and support them through the deep disappointment taking over their heart.

My mama heart may ache every time my child's heart breaks, but I guess for now I have to keep attempting to find the balance while continuously walking side by side with them on their path of life. That's all I can do.

When my kids are grown, I hope they know my arms will always be a safe place to land, my heart will always be accepting of who they are, and I will forever and always be available to wrap them up in the love they need.

Reflection

My heart breaks for my teen when. . .

Grace in the Dressing Room

Do you ever have one of those days you are pulled in a million directions?

Well, today was one of those days for me...

Prom dress shopping with one daughter, after picking another daughter up from an SAT, an hour away, while also watching two other daughters play volleyball, in two different tournaments, on a live stream, and if you are wondering where my husband was...he was at home scrubbing bathrooms and toilets while also watching the live stream!

Phew!

Sometimes trying to be there for all of them at the same time is exhausting. But you know what, that's okay by me.

Yes, there are days it's just a one on one with my girl, just us, no interruptions and laser focus. But then there are other days, I'm pulled in many directions for each of them and all I can do is try my best.

That is truly all I can do.

I try my best...

Wow! But some days are harder to manage and today was one of those days.

As I sat in the dressing room, I would watch the live streaming of the volleyball tournaments while she would change into another gorgeous gown.

Glasses on, watch game...
Glasses off, look up, marvel at my beautiful daughter in another gown, chat about it, give it a score, curtain closed...
Glasses on, watch game, and repeat.

For a moment, I was stressed she felt I wasn't all there, a bit of guilt taking over...

But as I explained what I was doing and why, my daughter didn't flinch, she didn't have a look of disappointment on her face and rather offered understanding and lots of grace.

I received a blessing today in the dressing room...

Grace...

She offered me grace so I didn't feel torn as a mama.

My daughter simply understood the need to be there for the other girls as well...even if it meant watching them on a live stream...

Because hey, that's what mamas do right?

We try our best to be a part of every moment for our children no matter how big or small.

So at the end of the day, sitting side-by-side at home, munching on burgers and fries after a few hours of shopping, my happy prom dress daughter and I continued to watch the live streaming together, cheering on her sisters. . . and I wouldn't trade it for the world.

> *Being a mother means continuing to spread your love even on the days you don't have much more to give. We need to believe in, continuously encourage, and show up for our children over and over again, day after day.*

Reflection

Ways I feel torn as a mom. . .

Breathe, Mama

Let the wind blow through you and cleanse all of your troubles.
Feel it swirl around you offering up a peace only you can understand.
Offer up to the wind your guilt, self-doubt, fears, and anxiety.
Offer up to the wind the one who questions everything.
Offer up the times with the kids where you lost your cool, said harsh words, and were less than patient.
Feel the swirling air hold you tight, as it hugs you, kissing your face and letting you know all will be okay.

Breathe, Mama.
Breathe.

As the wind keeps swirling and you keep moving forward, allow the breeze to fill your lungs up with hope, love, and new goals.

Let go of the old.
Take hold of your dreams.
Take hold of your fears and deepest desires.

See the good.
Your mistakes don't define you.

See the love.
Your children laughing and gazing at you is proof of your success.

See the joy.
Their smiles around tell a part of your story.

See the hope.
Your children growing up and navigating this world is breathtaking.

Soak it all in, Mama.

Yes, the wind keeps swirling and time keeps moving forward at a rapid pace but so do you.
Don't hold on too tight, it will only hold you back.

Soak it all in, Mama.

Allow the wind to hold you, as you continue to inhale and breathe new life into this big world, while offering up and cleansing the old.

Soak it all in, Mama.

Breathe, Mama.
Breathe.

> *There are days I question if I'm failing but every time my child comes in for a hug I know, in the belly of my soul, that I am exactly where I need to be in this season of motherhood and what a blessing it is to feel the love between a mother and a child.*

Reflection

A few tools and strategies that allow me to take hold of my breath and breathe...

There, I Said It

Some days I'm not patient or a good listener...there, I said it.
Some days I yell.
Some days I curse.
Some days I ignore or harbor anger built up inside of me.

Sometimes I'm not focused, I interrupt, and I offer too much advice, too soon, when all my teen wants me to do is listen.
I know that my teen needs me to listen and then listen some more.
She needs me to put it all down and give her my utmost attention.
She needs me to stop what I'm doing and listen with a clear heart and open mind.
She needs me to show up consistently with a lack of judgment.

But some days, I'm not patient or a good listener.

Some days I'm overwhelmed with all of the demands on my own life, and some days I am just downright exhausted.

But on the days I'm not patient; maybe I need some space, some time to clear my head, and work through what is mulling around up there. Or maybe I need a long walk meandering along the back road lined with organic grasses swaying in the wind, silently going through the twists and turns within my brain and the silly games it plays on me.

There, I Said It

You see, Mama, patience isn't always a given for me. Most days I have to work at it, and maybe you feel this way too.
I get overwhelmed by chaos.
I prefer some semblance of order.
I get frustrated by too much noise, and I prefer a soft lull to the air.

I get overwhelmed by a lot of people talking to me at once.
I prefer a one-on-one conversation that I can follow and give my attention to.
I get frustrated by feeling torn in a few directions, and I prefer focusing on one thing at a time.

So on the days my patience is dwindling or spiraling downhill and the days I just can't find it within myself to actively listen or engage in conversation, I need to acknowledge and make room for space.
Space for myself to regroup and recollect my thoughts and allow room for more patience to emerge for my teen.

But you know what doesn't change whether I'm being a good listener and patient or not, my teen is navigating this ever-changing world, within her ever-changing emotions, and she needs me to listen to the words she is pouring from her heart.
She needs me to listen to the secrets she holds within and shares with me in confidence.
She needs me to absorb and digest every word seriously, knowing her words matter.

So as tired as I am or as much as I want to resolve things for her in a quick fashion, I need to muster up, with every cell of my body, new ways to become a better listener.

Not a listener filled with distractions.
Not a listener who is scrolling on a phone and not a listener who is too busy making dinner that I can't set it all down to give my teen what she needs.

This motherhood thing is a long road of continuous learning, twists and turns, room for improvement and flexibility, while including patience and love at the same time and one thing I know for sure is that this mama is trying her hardest.

> *When my teen enters the room, I need to set it all down and look them in the eye so they know they have my attention and that their words matter. I need to offer them the space to open their heart to me, and the only way to do this is by truly listening and being present in the moment and not distracted by anything else.*

Reflection...

A few ways I can improve my patience or listening skills...

Blooms of Life

The hydrangeas in our yard have always been a sense of comfort for me, wrapping me up in happiness and a sense of love. It's a comfort of knowing that spring is upon us, as the small green buds appear, while knowing that the beautiful blooms of summer are right around the corner. As I get older and travel my motherhood journey, I have realized that the blooming buds are very similar to how I view my life with my children.

Just as the hydrangeas began as small plants that need a lot of tending to with the perfect amount of watering each day, while tender hands take care of every element, motherhood is quite similar.
Motherhood is moments filled with loads of grace, tremendous amounts of learning and pruning along the way, all while hoping and wishing for a beautiful bloom to emerge within a season of life.

So as the hydrangeas sprout each spring and the small green buds make their appearance, I can't help but also be reminded of how my children have evolved and grown throughout the year as well.

But you see, just like the harsh elements of the earth that the hydrangeas need to push through, the year of nurturing and growth isn't always enough or an easy season for our children either. Often it's a year full of hardship throughout the blustery days of fall or an icy patch throughout the winter months while still holding on, every so tightly, to the hope of what lay ahead. Growth.

Growth within ourselves.
Growth within our children.
Growth within our garden.

We may not see it right away and some days even silently question if we have done something wrong, but there is always an evolution. Maybe the blooms don't appear as dazzling and the purple hue seems duller than the year before, but new buds are appearing, leaves are sprouting, and wood keeps blooming more delicate petals each and every day. As the days get warmer and the growth seems to take hold, some years may simply be understated and not as vibrant.

Just like my children, I'm reminded that growth is slow. It can't be rushed.
It's a growth that requires patience and understanding, lots of love and tending to.
It's a growth that offers the course of change and acceptance of what becomes in that element of time.
It's a growth rooted in love.

As I journey through this new season, with all of my children now grown, I'm reminded of how beautiful the journey of motherhood was, and continues to be, as it fuels my soul with peace. So as I gaze out of the kitchen window, at the magnificent hydrangeas topped with dew droplets, I'm reminded of the breathtaking memories of my children growing up and the beautiful blessings that surround me as I greet the warm summer morning ahead.

May I let go of the idea that I need to be a perfect mother and rather embrace the imperfect mother I am today. A mother who is evolving alongside her children as she becomes the woman and mom her family needs her to be.

Reflection

A few ways I'm growing throughout my journey...

Climbing Uphill

The funny thing about raising teens is one moment they're online looking at the latest styles to buy, and the next they are walking up the driveway looking like the little girls who used to greet me each afternoon at the bus stop ready to run home and up their favorite hill.

You see, some things never change. Even though time moves on, the cascading hill my girls used to climb when they were younger, which led to a shortcut to the front door, is a path my teens will continue to choose rather than walking the remaining part of the driveway.

It's a shortcut they created as all four of them ran off of the bus every afternoon during elementary school. It's a hill, which at one point was probably considered a giant mountain, that started the afternoon out with a challenge, sometimes bragging rights, often tears, and scraped knees, but regardless of what happened while climbing uphill, the path always led to some long awaited hugs after a long day from me.

Each and every day, rain or shine, snow days or humid days, it was guaranteed that four backpacks were dropped in the dirt at the bottom of the hill and as I gathered the bags in my hand to carry up the driveway the girls began their descent uphill.

They navigated the overgrowth of weeds, and they helped the tentative ones up when it got too steep with words of encouragement and a hand to hold. They watched the oldest sister race up the hill as if it was her biggest goal to tackle that day and as they climbed over the rocky stone wall they knew the front door led to the comfort of home and my arms wrapping them in an embrace that only a mom can give.

The hill remains just as it always has, but it now reminds me not only of their daily decent but also the challenges of life, school, friendships, and all of the chaos that being a teen brings about. And every now and then as I gaze out of the window of the house, I see a glimpse of four young women climbing up the hill from the driveway and all I can do is smile. Because even as my little girls become young women, they are forever little girls at heart filling themselves up with the comforts of their childhood.

And maybe, just maybe, climbing that mountain every now and then is a reminder to lean into goals, challenge oneself, lend a helping hand to others, and always take the path that isn't so clearly laid out for them. Maybe the boulders leading to the safety of home, the opportunity to challenge oneself while being supported and loved knowing mom always follows with backpacks in hand and a front door opening up, reminds them they are truly never alone.

Motherhood is making peace within the chaos in order to create a childhood filled with love, where grown children long to find the road that always leads to home and open the door to loving arms embracing their return.

Reflection

A few ways our home offers love and never feeling alone...

My Motherhood Journey

The mom I am today is not who I thought I would be, and it took me a very long time to admit this truth without feeling guilty or bad about it.

I always thought I would be the fun-loving mom who laughs wildly and allows rules to fall by the wayside, similar to what I saw in the movies.
I would be easygoing with lots of time for deep conversations and always speaking calmly and patiently with my teens.
Well, I was wrong. Dead, stop wrong!
I am not always that mom.

This motherhood gig is really hard some days, and on those days I often feel defeated.

Maybe I raised my voice, lost my patience, or didn't see eye to eye with my daughter.

Maybe I needed some time alone to think as I was feeling suffocated by everything I'm expected to keep track of.

Or maybe my expectations of what being a mom was going to be like truly isn't what is happening in reality and a sadness takes over.

Maybe on my very best day I can get to the point of being the mom I thought I would be, but most days I am hyperfocused on matters that my kids think don't really matter and as they would say are "not that deep" yet I focus on these issues until it's smooshed to a pulp and a big mess.

I don't always move forward, and I get trapped in a well of worry and nerves and do I dare mention the lack of sleep over these matters?

I can barely keep my thoughts aligned, and on most days I even tend to forget most of my thoughts because so much brain fog has set in.
My thoughts aren't necessarily reflective about life and pondering but rather wondering and often worrying how I am going to cram into my day all that needs to get done and if I will even slightly fulfill all of the needs of my children.

Conversations with my teen is often in the car driving from one place to another frantically trying to get there on time. On our good days our drive is lively and filled with fine details that I missed along the way, but other days silence takes over the once joyful car ride, and it's filled with grunts and a deep feeling of dread knowing how hard it is being a teenager in our world today.

My patience has been missing for some time now and honestly, I'm quietly waiting for it to return so I can make another attempt to be the mom I yearn to be.

But Mama, you know what I have realized as time moves on and I gather more wisdom throughout my time being a mom?
It's not easy being a mom.
It's not easy raising a teen.
It's not easy to take on the load of your daily life and your kids' stuff also.

But what I do know is this...

I'm a mom who gives her all and even more, and I'm a mom who loves and loves hard. I'm a mom who worries and worries hard, and I'm a mom who stands by and doesn't back down.
So I may not be the perfect mom, and I may not always be the mom I envisioned I would be, but life has taught me that I'm the mom my kids need me to be and I wouldn't change a thing.
Good days.
Bad days.
Days that feel effortless and days filled with the ugliest parts of our journey.
All of it matters.
All of it means something.
And all of it creates who I am as a mother, and I don't have an ounce of guilt for who this woman and mother has turned out to be.

So Mama, continue to offer yourself a clean slate. Each morning as the sun rises breathe in, breathe out, and keep moving forward on your breathtaking, beautiful, and sometimes brutal pathway of your unique motherhood journey.

To the mama struggling while raising her teen but continues to show up day after day, you are doing a wonderful job. Your commitment to your family is seen and your love doesn't go unnoticed.

Reflection

Simple changes I have made along my journey as a mom...

Remember When?

Remember when pudgy feet ran down the hallway and pink plastic princess shoes tapped throughout the house?

Remember when Greg Wiggle was an icon and a hug and a kiss cured everything?

Remember when life was simpler building forts for hours upon hours while every sheet and blanket found in the linen closet went missing and catching frogs in the early morning in jammies, feet wet and covered in mud meant everything?

Remember when the yellow school bus meant feeling like a big kid as you tentatively climbed the looming steps to take your seat and carpools filled with friends allowed me a glimpse into the teenage world?

Remember when life wasn't rushed frantically running from place to place and daydreaming on the lawn talking about cloud formations slowed down time?

Remember when catching fireflies in the night sky during the early days of summer and staying up late to roast marshmallows created summer memories to last a lifetime and sleepovers were made of late night giggles holding tight to cupcake pillow?

I hope and pray I always remember.

Now as I watch you grow and unfold into the teenager before me, standing taller than me with beautiful confidence, I find myself saying a silent prayer to never forget one moment.

I hope and pray I always remember your sweet smile as you parted your lips to reveal your two top missing teeth.
I hope and pray I always remember the way your blonde pigtails would blow in the wind as you pedaled your pretty pink princess bike down the driveway.
I hope and pray I always remember your high-pitched laughter echoing through every inch of the house and down every hallway.

I hope and pray...

I hope and pray, that now as a teen, I always remember how you are finding your way and embarking on your own path and journey containing all of your life goals and desires.

I hope and pray I always remember your soft hand in mind gently holding on, while squeezing tightly in stressful times.

I hope and pray I always remember your eloquent words as you share your most hidden secrets and words of hope as you grow up in a world filled with chaos.

I hope and pray...

I hope and pray I always remember your arms wrapped around me in a hug for no reason at all except to silently reassure me that our bond is tightly woven and our connection will never be severed.

I hope and pray I always remember the stories you share that lighten my mood lift my spirits and fill up my heart.

I hope and pray I always remember how your sweet and tender soul touches the hearts of everyone you meet.

I hope and pray...

I hope and pray I always remember how you will forever make an imprint on my heart, no matter how old I am.

As gray hair highlights my once chocolate brown mane and wrinkles create fine lines in a crevice around my eyes, may I always remember the feeling that you have left upon my heart.

When the day arrives and my memory doesn't serve me well and I struggle to come up with the words, may the family albums, created with love, bring me back to these precious memories.

Memories of the children who gave me life on the day they were born yet take my breath away each and every time they grace the room.
And may these memories, printed on paper and stored away in a box, now aged with time, fill my heart as I gaze at each one with the laughter that once filled our home and as I sort through each and every sepia photograph may I be reminded of a life well spent raising my children.

And may I continue to feel, no matter how old I may be the feeling of love, deep in my soul, that is never too far away and tucked into a special part of my heart. A special area reserved solely for me.

The heart of a mother.

I hope and pray. . .

> *Being a mother unlocked parts of myself I never knew existed. It opened me up to a love I never dreamed possible and a hope to make all things right. Motherhood breathed life directly into this heart of mine and offered me a love like no other.*

Reflection

My hopes and prayers as life moves forward. . .

More Mistakes

I make a lot of mistakes and one of my daughters, ever so kindly, brought a few of my mistakes to my attention last night.

She is feeling a disconnect and wants our relationship to quickly repair, so we can go back to our fun-loving relationship, not the one lately, which is filled with dirt, grime, and all things pulling us down.

But to resolve and restore us, we need to dig deep, lay it all out there and get right down to the ugly parts. Yuck. . . I hate those deep-rooted ugly parts that often need to be dug out from the depths to see the light, but we had to buckle up and get to digging.

So, we dug. . .
and we dug some more.

Mama, some parts may have been hard to digest and swallow, I admit, but it's exactly what my ears needed to hear.

I will make mistakes and I will continue to mess up today, tomorrow, and many days to come but I am human and I have to be okay with mistakes.

But what I can't be is complacent when my daughter reaches out to talk openly about a few things that need to change.

I also can't help but remind her that I'm human.

Everyday I try but sometimes I just need a gentle nudge letting me know that I have not been myself, to own my mistakes, move forward, and get back to the light.

Mistakes happen. . . I'm human.

But the love emanating from my daughter's sweet soul allows me to close my eyes each night, knowing tomorrow is a new day, hopefully filled with one less mistake and my light shining ever so brightly again.

I make mistakes, I'm human, and so are you.

Moms make mistakes and we don't always know what to say, but I hope my children know just how much their mother loves them even on the hardest of days.

Reflection

Mistakes I have made along the way. . .

Mama

Mama,

You will be disappointed.
You will feel the weight of the world on your shoulders, but you will also be wrapped in love.

You will feel betrayed at times and lonely.
You will feel left out, but you will always be wrapped in love.

You will feel life isn't always easy and friends flow like the changing tide.
You will feel pressure from the outside world telling you that you are not enough but hold close to your heart that you will always be wrapped in love.

You will fall prey to the comparison trap.
You will wonder why sometimes.
You will question your decisions made and you will always be wrapped in love.

You will give compassion to others but may not always receive it back.
You will find kindness in those you meet on your path and you will always be wrapped in love.

You will feel joy.
You will feel turmoil.
And your heart strings will be tugged when you least expect it, but you will always be wrapped in love.

Because you see, Mama, you are the darkness in the light, the joy within the sorrow, and you are the consistent force guiding your child on a path of love.

> *Motherhood is life altering but no one shared with me how watching my children grow up would take an emotional toll on my heart, leaving me breathless some days gasping for air, yet still coming to the surface to take my next breath.*

Reflection

Some things that have been pressing on my heart lately...

Some Days Are Hard

It's hard being a mom.
I'm just sitting here by myself thinking about all the mistakes that I've made, all of the times that maybe I could've kept quiet, the times I could've said more, the times I needed to speak but my teen didn't want to hear what I had to say.

All of the times I have had to run to the bathroom to gather my composure, to run cold water on my wrists to bring down my anxiety, to look at myself in the mirror and take a deep breath to hold back the tears, because I felt disconnected.

I sit here thinking about what I want for the future, how to have it while thinking what I'm doing is right, but so often it's dead wrong, thinking about how to support my teen the best I can but at the same time, not knowing anything at all and feeling like I should know more, do more, be more, but to be honest with you I'm doing all that I possibly can, while every element and every cell in my body is devoted to my children, but it still never feels like enough.

Why doesn't it ever feel like enough?

I know what I'm doing is enough.

I know I go above and beyond but why does it feel like it's not enough?
Why does it feel this way?

And then I sit here and I wonder, am I the only one who feels this way as a mom?

Am I alone on this journey?
Am I alone thinking I don't know where this is going to land?
But what I do know is this…

Some mornings call for an extra cup of something.

Some mornings need an excess of hugs and kisses before walking out the door.

Some mornings run smoothly without any bumps and some mornings it's a chore to get out of bed.

Some mornings I'm cheerful and optimistic and some mornings I carry the weight of all those around me.

Some mornings I really love hard and some mornings I need to be loved harder.

Some mornings I need to feel the ache of letting go and some mornings I'm filled to the brim watching my big kids soar on their path.

But even on the days, I feel down in the trenches of motherhood and being sucked further down the rabbit hole of life, I'm hopeful for the future.
I'm hopeful for an adult relationship with my teen even though some days we don't see eye to eye.

Some Days Are Hard

I wonder if I am in an awkward phase of motherhood or if my teenagers and college kids are in a stage where they are yearning to be independent and on their own, but yet still holding on and needing me to help guide them through certain elements of life.

Mama, this journey is a learning space for everyone, both my teens and myself, and the more I am open to this truthful honesty the better I can navigate being a mom through the teen years.

It's hard being a mom and sometimes, Mama, we just need to word vomit and get it the truth out there. We need to share with transparency how difficult it truly can be and allow other moms to know they are not alone.

So Mama, you are not alone if today you had to look at yourself in the mirror and settle your breath, settle your heart, and settle feeling not good enough in order to put one foot in front of the other. And maybe, just maybe, knowing this truth we can get through this stage of our motherhood journey together because I know I need all of the support I can get. You are not alone.

> *Be gentle with yourself, Mama. You are challenged in ways you never knew and you are trying each day to be the very best mom you can be. Believe in yourself that you are enough. Be gentle with the mother you are because she deserves to feel loved too.*

Reflection

Offering up, with complete honesty, ways that I'm not feeling enough...

One Rose and a Thorn

How did we go from two highs and one low sitting around the dinner table, all six of us, giggling about our days, the conversation always being initiated by me, and now as we walk along the pier my girl is asking me on my birthday, "Mom, what is your one rose and one thorn for this year?"

As these words escaped her lips and the sun shone brightly on my face, I took a breathless pause and quietly exhaled as a smile crossed my face and my memory took me back to those moments surrounding the often chaotic farm table. My footsteps may have been moving forward but I was lost in time for a few seconds before I could muster up any words to share my heart.

I was brought back in time to those dinner conversations, a little gesture each evening as we slowed down around the table and recalled how much she used to enjoy this game. She would clap her hands loudly with excitement, giggle with joy, and shed tears some nights as she shared a heartache from that day. As a little girl she played two highs and one low but now this game, with a new title, is her grown-up version. A version she now incorporates into her life as a grown woman living in a college apartment with the friends she calls family.

This moment, with the sun shining on the placid bay made me realize how blessed I am to be a mom. It's moments like this that reassure me that I did something right. We may have had our family challenges, but this moment in time with the sun beaming on our faces, talking about our roses and thorns of the year, is exactly what I've always wished for.

A wish for my daughters to incorporate some of those little family traditions from their childhood into their life. It doesn't have to be exactly how I did it but incorporating those emotional connections and ties that bind a family together will forever melt my heart.

"So, Mom, you still haven't answered. What's your rose?"
And with a softness in my voice, holding back the shakiness that could make way for some tears, I shared, "My rose is seeing you and your sisters accomplish all of the dreams and goals that you have set for yourselves. It doesn't mean that I don't have my own personal rose to cherish, but you girls will always be my rose, each and every year, for as long as I am breathing."

> *Mothers don't get another chance at raising their children; therefore, I'm focusing on fostering stronger connections with my kids. One day the daily interactions will be gone, the house will empty out, and silence will take over my weary mama heart. So today, I'm focusing on us, and only us, everything else can wait for these moments of connection are priceless.*

Reflection

My rose and thorn for today...

Lean In

Hey Mama,
Lean in and listen... I have a little secret to share with you.

Do you know how moms are often scared for the teen years to arrive?
Well, it's not as bad as you think and I want to share with you this truth.

Now don't get me wrong, this doesn't mean I didn't have hard times with my girls. Trust me, there were days I was barely catching my breath, and hoping I could find a simple way to either reconnect with them or have this stage move forward as fast as possible. I would often wish I was Knight Rider traveling in my black car, KITT, at lighting speed to get to the next destination yet my black car never showed up ready to scoop me away and rescue me. But no matter how hard I wished this stage away, I realized I had to stay put.

We hear over and over again from the media that the teen years are going to plummet us moms into a cycle of obnoxious behavior with our teen, combined with disrespect, lots of eye rolls, and slammed doors spewing profanities. But you know what?
After teaching teenagers and raising four girls, all in high school at the same time, I can assure you that it's long overdue for this fear to be laid to rest.

Yes, teens will have their moments, and yes, we are going to lose our cool, but I believe the stigma surrounding teens is dramatic and not quite fair to them if I'm being honest.

Even as moms, we have days we aren't on our best behavior and can be obnoxious and rude. This is life. It doesn't mean it's a constant for years to come, and now imagine being told this is how you're supposed to behave once the pre-teen years arrive? Our kids hear, read, watch on TV and this message being portrayed. The perspective needs to shift in order for our teens to believe that even on the hard days, being a teen can also be filled with beauty and magic.

As moms, we also need to believe that this season of motherhood can be beautiful as both our teen and ourselves evolve and experience tremendous growth along the way.

You see, Mama, our teens are magical humans with pure hearts ready to take on the world.

They need us to support them as their minds wander and encourage them along the way believing that they will make a difference in our world.

They need us to listen to their hearts that are filled with hope and knowledge for the future, because they are our future leaders. They are the ones we need to put our trust and complete faith in because the reality is these hormonal humans, changing every day, are the ones who are going to impact the world for the better.

But to accomplish this evolution during this season, they need us to hold them close as they travel through unknown territories on their journey, allowing them to explore, develop, and sometimes fail miserably. But most importantly, they need us to provide this support with an unwavering amount of unconditional love that is bound together with grace and forgiveness.

As I read my own words and reflect, I'm thrown back to a time where raising four girls in high school was not easy. There were days I felt I couldn't make everyone happy, there was a tremendous amount of arguing, and days where I felt completely disconnected when all I was yearning for was connection. I had read all of the parenting books out there and had two degrees in education with multiple classes on attachment and parenting, yet why did I feel so incredibly disconnected? But then there were days filled with laughter echoing off every wall of our home and tears of happiness, words of encouragement, and copious amounts of hugs and kisses.

But still, some days I felt stuck. We weren't always disconnected, but I was able to see a pattern. I realized this feeling really had nothing to do with my daughters; it was about me.

I had to let go.
I was holding on too tight and my girls were fighting me on it.
I was too much in their business and at times they were pushing me away and I was in a constant state of wanting to always be by their side and therefore, I was suffocating everyone.

So you know what I slowly started to do?
I started to recognize the truth.
My girls weren't teens filled with hostility. They were young woman feeling trapped, seeking independence, yet didn't know how to go about it or how to ask for it. They were young women wanting to remain children but wanting to explore new territories. And with this knowledge, I slowly and with a great ache in my heart began to let go.

But let's be clear, Mama, letting go doesn't mean severing all connections.
Letting go, for me, meant one thing. Allowing my daughters the freedom to begin to create their own path. The path that is meant for them, not the path I envisioned for them and a path that only they can travel.

And in time, our relationships turned around.
Gone were the days of arguing multiple times each day because we were in a power struggle. My daughters began coming to me and sharing their hearts, goals, and dreams. They began to let me in and once I opened the door beautiful connections began.

You see, Mama, the act of our teens growing up and entering this stage isn't the hard part, it's how we respond to it. I truly believe if we shift our perspective to one where we find the light and offer up grace, maybe, just maybe, the eye rolls will come to an end and connection will once again be found.

> *The best part of being a mom is knowing my teen finally understands that I am their person supporting, loving, encouraging, and validating them along the way. When they realize they are my everything and I would do anything for them, the door opens up for a stronger connection, linking us arm in arm for life.*

Reflection

My teen is struggling with. . .
I am struggling with. . .

Fighting Little Fires

Do you ever feel like you're putting out little fires day in and day out?

I do, and it's exhausting.
As a mom, I get it, this is a part of my job, but holy moly I didn't ever expect this feeling.

Why are there so many little fires surrounding me?
Where is my lifeline?
Why do I feel trapped within the smoke of the fire and feel like I can't escape?

These fires are suffocating me while the rising smoke riddles my space without a clear exit in sight.

It's filling me up, with each inhalation, and enters my lungs taking over until I'm forcefully holding my breath not knowing where to turn or what to do.

And then. . .I miraculously exhale.
Where did this come from?
As I take a deep breath and exhale, I know that in due time my unsteady breath will steady itself.

But in those moments, in the midst of it all barely breathing and on the ground, I know I need to reach out for help or this suffocating feeling may linger on forever.

Mama, it's so hard to admit that some days motherhood is hard. It's hard to accept the truth and admit that motherhood is beautiful and brutal while still allowing yourself to feel that you are a good mom.
But the reality of motherhood is knowing there is beauty even within the little fires that pop up sometimes daily, other times weekly or monthly, yet always sporadically surprise us.
Through it all, though, the little fires always come to an end no matter how small or massive they may be.

And here's the truth, if I have learned anything on my journey as a mom, the little fires are almost always resolved, and I can always breathe once again.
Mama, even through the hard, there is new breath and life within each new day and lessons to be learned.

The little fires don't need to consume, suck me down, or take over as smoke billows around; rather, they can guide me to show my kids how to deal with life's struggles, one moment at a time, while teaching them strength, tenacity, resilience, and grace.

Because you see, Mama, as I continue on my path, raising teens, I will pull up all of the grace inside of me, take a step forward as I exhale, and allow the dust to once again settle around me, because as we know, it always does.

A mother is a warrior sacrificing beyond measure to create a life for her child that goes beyond anything she has ever dreamed possible.

Reflection

Ways I put out little fires to create more space for peace. . .

A Peaceful Drive

As I look over toward the passenger's seat and catch a glimpse of my growing teen, a sense of peace comes over me.

As I drive the open road, I feel connected to my daughter in a way that I don't always experience at home while sitting on the couch side-by-side. It's as if she transforms into a different person when she slides into the leather seats and closes the passenger door.

All of a sudden she wants to be taken care of again. She relaxes, and the stressors of life seem to disappear.
She doesn't want to be the driver even though she has her license, and within minutes, sometimes seconds, the doors of conversation opens up. She goes into a confessional, sharing her secrets, what's been troubling her heart, and goals she has for her future self as the radio quietly plays her favorite song.

Some days our car rides are filled with silence, not a word spoken, sometimes a tone of frustration seeps in, and other times a contagious giggle fills up the car with peace and joy. Knowing the car is a place for her to feel connected to me though enables me to breathe as I recall with great clarity how difficult this time in life can be.

Mama, I have learned a lot on our countless car rides. I used to think in order to feel connected my daughter and I needed to bond over big moments. But honestly, what I have realized is it's the simple moments, the ordinary times driving in my sweatpants with a messy bun and slippers doing a late night pick up, early morning drive to school, or running a quick errand where we are most connected.

It's the little moments that mean the most, and I don't take them lightly. As these moments creep in and seep into my life, I try my best to incorporate them as often as possible. Sometimes I'll notice that my teen is struggling but remaining quiet so I'll suggest a drive. Usually within minutes her shoes are on, and as she walks toward the car I feel her relax, knowing the car is her safe place to share her heart and as the doors close she becomes wrapped in her safe haven confessional and I feel blessed.

Mama, it may seem silly but right now if you are feeling a disconnect with your teen, ask them to run an errand or grab some coffee. Once you open up that door, you may be surprised at what comes barreling out and shared, creating a beautiful connection in the confines of a car.
Who knew that the car, a simple vehicle getting me from point A to point B could fill up my mama heart with so much peace and renewal and maybe a simple drive can do this for you too.

> *And just like that the open road led to a space where secrets didn't exist and sharing our hearts led to a connection that words could never explain.*

Reflection

A few ways my teen and I reconnect on a drive. . .

Chaos and Truth

The chaos of my daughter's junior year has tested me in ways I didn't know was even possible. As I sit up late at night worrying about and ruminating on all of the thoughts consuming me, I wonder if other moms feel the same. I feel torn in a multitude of directions and sad for my daughter because if I'm feeling this way and not actually living in it, then I can only imagine how she is feeling. She is stressed out beyond belief, and I honestly don't recall feeling this way at 16 years old.

I don't recall feeling a heavy weight on my shoulders, pushing me further and further down, as I attempted with all of my might to stay afloat. But then again, a lot of our teens are being bogged down by more academically rigorous classes. And why is it that in one school year our teens are learning to drive, studying for standardized tests, taking high-level classes while also keeping up friendships, and potentially trying to sneak in a family dinner here and there while getting to extracurricular activities to then be followed up with volunteer hours.
Honestly, Mama, I'm worn out and tired from simply watching my daughter navigate all of this.

I don't know how she hasn't yet self-combusted. I mean, let's be honest, really honest with one another. This is way too much of a load for our teens to carry and it makes sense to me that as moms, we often take on some of our teens' emotional stress and put it onto ourselves. It's a lot to haul around each day without adding on hours to the day. I can't quite describe the intense feeling of overwhelm that floats through the air of our house while worrying if she is doing the right thing and feeling an ache in my soul that this truly isn't how my daughter should be living her life and maybe you are feeling some of this too.

Where are the days of scrambling home from school to complete an insignificant amount of homework before heading out again to meet up with friends? Where are the days where parties took place in the woods but cops weren't called? Where are the days of creating mixed tapes and spending countless hours in a bedroom making collages for a friend's birthday while listening attentively to the radio to press record at the exact moment to get just the right song to add to the mixed tape? And where are the days where rigorous classes didn't control a teenager's life?

Maybe I'm old, but I miss these carefree days, and I find that when I'm unwinding in bed at night quietly thinking, I yearn for my daughter to live a simpler life with less cut-throat competition and a life that she fondly looks back on. But, Mama, I'm concerned and scared. I feel our teens have too much pressure overall and their childhood is being stripped away from them way too early, but I also know this reality will most likely not change.

So all I can do is hold my girl tight, tell her over and over again her hard work will pay off, and validate and agree with her that this weight she carries is just too much. Mama, it's all I can do, and if your son or daughter is a teen in the thick of this too, just hold them. Remind them that this pressure they feel right now isn't normal, and with time the load will lighten, and maybe in the near future there will be a change.

A change to let childhood last a bit longer where being 16 is simple and not filled with test scores, high-level classes, or likes and comments from social media. Because the truth is, as moms, we just want our teen to be filled with love where all of the above doesn't even matter.

> *As I gaze at my teen, I am silently cheering for her, filling her up with the confidence she needs to take on the world and not fall into the comparison trap. I pray she loves and accepts herself for who she is, the breathtaking woman looking back at her in the mirror each day.*

Reflection

My teen is having a hard time right now with. . .
And
I'm having a hard time right now with. . .

Decisions, Decisions

Sometimes we have to hold on and give ourselves permission to feel it all, and today was one of those days.

Today I heard the voice of my sweet girl say the words, "Mom, I made my decision."

Is it possible the butterflies I felt on her first day of kindergarten, as she stood in my kitchen, sucking her thumb, wearing her polka dot pink dress, so quickly came flooding back in full force?

Is it possible to feel a deep ache and extreme joy at the same time, as my first baby, pressed the accept button, finalizing the decision for the university she will call home in the fall?

Well, my heart is aching a bit, for what will change and how time wasn't as slow as I had hoped, but to be honest, the butterflies in my stomach have not stopped fluttering all day, and I'm embracing it.

Flutter. . .a peace that touches every ounce of my core, in a fast yet gentle way, reminding me of the first flutters I felt while newly pregnant.

Flutter. . .excitement for what is to come on her beautiful journey and the lives she will touch with her compassionate heart.

Flutter…a pang of guilt for some of the times we didn't get along or argued over the small stuff.

Flutter…our home will be quieter, the laundry lighter, and the table soon set for five, not six…rapid flutter.

Flutter…our home will miss her smile, the car will be in the garage until another new driver moves up the ranks, and my ears will not hear her voice calling out to me each time she leaves.

Her wings are not subtly fluttering rather they are ready, prepared, and about to take flight. And once she takes flight, I am confident she will place her mark on the world and soar.

So maybe, Mama, I need to accept the flutters, give in and feel each and every one, knowing and trusting she has made a sound decision for where she envisions her path to take her along her journey of life.

And maybe the flutters remind me to take pause while I anticipate her departure and watch my sweet girl, with such ease and grace gradually take flight while I continue to look on, as my heart flutters with wonder and awe.

> *It doesn't matter if my teen is going to college, the military, or another path. As a mom, I will always worry about them until my very last breath. It's who I am.*

Reflection

Something that is making my heart flutter lately…
And
A big decision my teen has recently made…

Don't Give Up On Me, Mama
Love, Your Teen

Don't give up on me, Mama.
Please don't give up on me.
Please don't quit.
I need you.

I know you're worried about me and you feel the weight of the world on your shoulders surrounding my emotional needs right now.
I know we're not seeing eye to eye and we are struggling through every bump in the road of our relationship. And I know I'm lashing out and fighting you on everything, but please, Mama don't give up on me.

I see the tears rolling down your face from frustration, sadness, and loneliness as I push you away and I hear my door slam as I scream out "I hate you," but please, Mama, don't give up on me.

I know my laundry is all over the floor, my room is a mess, and you can't find your forks, spoons, or water bottles, and I know

Don't Give Up On Me, Mama

you've asked me to pick things up and be more respectful of our home and not let the chaos take over, but for some reason right now it all feels so overwhelming.
Every little thing is taking over my brain, and I can barely focus, but please, Mama, don't give up on me.

When I push you away, I know it hurts your heart, and I see that you keep pushing through, but I know it's hard for you. I know you muster up all of your energy to continue to have conversation, make my favorite dinners, do late-night carpool pickups, and attend every activity and event that I am in. I see you. You keep showing up, and I don't say anything but please, Mama, don't give up on me.

I can see as you look into my eyes how much you love me, even though venomous words exit my mouth and I'm spiraling out of control, but please, Mama, promise me you will never give up on me.

You always show up.
You always offer a helping hand.
You always love unconditionally.

I feel your love, Mama.
I'm soaking it all in.
I'm absorbing it.
Just know, Mama, each night as I lay my head on the pillow I close my eyes knowing one person in this world will never give up on me.
Thank you, Mama.

Love,
Your Teen

One thing I know for sure is that I will never regret the countless years, months, weeks, days, hours, minutes, or seconds I spent with my child.

Reflection

A promise to keep.
I will never give up on my teen even when…

Life Changes

Mama,
Do you ever have one of those days, weeks, or months where life is smooth sailing with your teen and the next day you are slammed with something you didn't envision coming your way?

When this happens to me, I often think somewhere in our being, deep within each of us, there is a desire to hide.

The need to retreat, run away, or pull back from life's problems...

The need to feel comfort within ourselves and our own surroundings...

The need to escape reality, with the hope that reality isn't the truth and only a manifestation of one day that changed the course of a lifetime...

So when these feelings take over, I know I have a lot of work to do.

I need to remind myself to stay as connected with my teen as possible and be as strong as my body will allow.
I have to relinquish control, while remaining grounded and still connected to my own being, accepting the darkest of times but knowing there is always a new day tomorrow.

But sometimes, Mama, I'm not as strong as I think I am.

Oftentimes I start to become unraveled and this is when I ask for strength and patience.

If these two attributes then latch onto me and encompass my being, then maybe my inner world that's spinning around with me teen will slow down.

But here's the thing, Mama, no matter how broken I may feel or disconnected with my teen, or caught off guard by them spiraling downward, my hope is for strength to be able to lift my face toward the sunshine of tomorrow.

My hope is for patience to be willing to accept, forgive, and move forward along my path.

Because with each new day, life continues to move forward whether it's one of those days, weeks, or months my teen and I are connected or disjointed.

The sun rises each morning.
The birds sing.
The flowers bloom.
The dreamers dream.
Children grow up.
More wrinkles appear, and life moves on with its dramatic beauty.

And as for me, I slowly begin to emerge.

Mama, even during the hardest of times, may we all find the strength to lift our face toward the sunshine of tomorrow, because no one ever said raising a teen was easy, and it's within the many blessings of tomorrow we can see the hope of the new day.

*I wish someone would have told me that as a mom,
it's okay to have hard days.
It's okay to cry.
It's okay to want to hide and escape and it's okay to feel it all.
But most of all I wish someone would have told me to always
remember to look toward the light and the hope of tomorrow.
Because, Mama, there is always hope in tomorrow.*

Reflection

Something that has been hard with my teen lately. . .

Being a mom is sending silent prayers of comfort and love to your child each and every day no matter how old they are.

PART

Letting Go

I'm that mom now who gazes at another mom in the grocery store, with a young baby, and silently thinks hold on it goes so fast, while at the same time thinking how breathtaking watching my children grow up truly is.

Introduction for Letting Go

Well, Mama, here we are.
I've been thinking a lot lately about letting go, what it entails, and how truly hard it can be. To be honest, this is the chapter of my motherhood journey that I have not been looking forward to but if I'm being completely transparent, I have been dreading it.

I've always known that I'm a very sentimental and nostalgic mom, but never in my wildest dreams did I ever think that the idea of my girls growing up would take hold of my heart as much as it has done. I often find myself staring at the breathtaking adults they are becoming, and even though I see the beauty in who they will be, I can't help but simultaneously wish to go back in time, even if just for one moment.

This motherhood gig is a constant push and pull, the ying and yang of my daily life, and some days I feel overwhelmed by the overwhelming amount of emotions that I feel.
I'm excited for the future and what's to become for my kids, yet I am also drowning in nostalgia because time flew by too fast for my liking.

I often wonder as I gaze into their eyes,
Where has the time gone?
How did it slip by so fast?
Did I miss out on certain things that I should have held tight too?
Was I the mom that they needed me to be for all of these years?
Have I done enough for them?
Have I loved them enough?

Letting Go

I slowly began the "letting go season" as they entered the teen years by offering more independence for time to reflect on themselves and who they wanted to become, and I now find myself holding on to those memories of their childhood as they begin to embark on their individual journeys of leaving home. The "letting go season" is coming to an end as my nest is emptying out, and I'm not quite sure how I feel about it.

But here we are.
As I sit gazing out the window, in the kitchen that holds countless memories, with my hot cup of chai latte, I wonder, how is it possible, that just like that, all of my girls are off in college, shoes aren't piled high by the door anymore, and the house is eerily quiet?

Is it possible that I just accomplished four college drop-offs in less than a week?
Is it normal that I felt my mind spinning out of control as I sat motionless on the plane flying back to an empty house not knowing what to expect, while worrying that I won't like this chapter of life one bit?

But on one of my first afternoons home, after all of the college drop-offs, not knowing what to do with myself, I ventured into town. Walking into the local pizzeria searching for some comfort, through a greasy slice, Caesar salad, and a Diet Coke, I was caught off guard and surprised to find that the guy working behind the counter became a balm to my soul that rainy day.

It was a simple interaction, "Where are all the girls? You're always with the girls."
And right then and there, as I stood gazing through the clear glass deciding which slice to choose, I realized that after 21 years of raising children, I was alone. Alone with my heart aching as my mind

wandered back to cutting up their pizza into tiny bite-size pieces so they wouldn't choke and alone in counting down the days until I shared a meal with them again. But in my despair I also realized something. I was alone but not lonely. For the first time in a long time one of the four girls wasn't standing by my side, and I knew this would take some getting used to, but I wasn't lonely. I had the company of myself to carry me through this new chapter of my life, and I knew with time my heart would feel full once again.

After a few days, I started to feel something deep within. My girls' happiness overrode the ache my heart felt within our goodbye, and I slowly began to allow myself to move forward, waking up with a smile on my face.

But Mama, let's face it. Letting go rattles us. Letting go tears us apart. And letting go made me fall down the rabbit hole of the movie reel of and my time raising children. My early days empty nesting felt like a constant movie playing over and over again of their childhood. The toothless girls bike riding in their princess dresses, picnics on the beach eating sugary doughnuts, quiet moments snuggled in a chair singing lullabies, and dance parties. So many dance parties. But what I realized during this time of reflection is this. . .letting go is part of child rearing all along, but as moms, we just don't talk about it much or focus on that part of motherhood.

You see, Mama, letting go is not easy nor is it the most natural thing we are encountering on our motherhood journey. As moms we are a constant in our kids' lives, and then in what seems like a split second they reach an age where one day life changes and it's time to let go. We all know it's a natural progression of growing up, but it's not necessarily natural for us moms to go through the act of letting go. And the worst part is we are expected to be okay with it, put a smile on our face and move on, but in truth many of us are breaking down and falling apart throughout this process and new chapter.

As a mom who often over-thinks and over-analyzes things, my mind races in the wee hours of the night, wondering what the future holds.

Am I going to be the one that they pick up the phone to call when they're bored or have a question?
Am I going to be the one they seek out for guidance and validation when they feel that there is no one else?
Because you see, this has been my goal all along while raising my kids and I can only hope that what I have done and continue to do is enough.

There are days this chapter of letting go is harder than others and there are days my wandering anxious mind takes over and I feel a loss of control, but all I can do is hope.

I will never know if what I'm doing is right but what I do know is when the phone rings and I hear on the other end, "Hi, Mom," my heart melts.

You see, Mama, that's all I want.
I want to hear, "Hi, Mom," until my very last breath and you may feel this way too.

Even though this new chapter of life is different and I'm adjusting to the new normal of empty nesting, I need to remember I'm still a mom and always will be no matter how old my girls are. I need to remind myself in those times of sadness, that my job as a mom is not over but rather my role has simply changed. I've accepted the fact that my heart is going to ache some days, but I will be okay because letting go isn't about me, it's about my kids. It's about encouraging my grown kids to thrive on their own and embrace the new chapter that they are embarking on with my love and support never wavering and remaining a constant.

So, Mama, may you once again know you are not alone as you also adjust to the many new beginnings coming your way as you travel your new journey of letting go.
Allow yourself the grace to feel it all. This is a time filled with many emotions that will consume you and suffocate you at times. But know that it's okay to feel these emotions. It's okay to feel lost in a moment as nostalgia takes over.
It's okay to cry for what is lost at the same time you are cheering for what is to come.
It's okay to miss when your kids where younger while relishing in who they are becoming.
And most importantly, it's okay to embrace this new chapter in your life through tears and a smile on your face all at the same time.

Hang in there, Mama. You've got this!

If I knew how fast time would go by, I would have slowed down a bit more. I would have soaked in more moments to hold onto once you were grown. I would have realized some moments simply don't matter and all that's important is feeling loved.

Last Moments

You know the days where you think your kiddos are never going to get of out diapers or pull-ups?

You know the days when you wonder if it's the last day they take a nap and maybe the last day you are able to shower without interruption?

Or the days when you hear your little one call, "Mama, or mommy, ma, or mom," over and over again and some days it melts your heart and other days you don't want to hear your name ever again?

You know those days where you drive around place to place, picking up at a friend's house, driving from one activity to another, stopping to get take out, and after an hour or two of being in the car you need to stop for a fountain soda to keep you going?

Or the days during the car rides you hear all the drama that goes on during study hall, the major break up of the year, or the stress of the huge bio test in a few days?

Those days come to an end and for me I am at the gusp of those moments ending.
These moments take me off guard and cause my heart to beat a bit faster as I'm filled with a bittersweet blend of nostalgia and

anticipation, marking the end of an era and the beginning of a new chapter.

My heartstrings have been tugged at throughout the course of my daughter's senior year whether it's the last time on a court, field, or stage, or the last award ceremony or concert attended. All of these moments are memories of who my daughter once was and who she will become in the years to come as she embarks on her journey.

Since my toothless little one stepped foot on the big yellow bus for the first day of kindergarten, memories are ingrained within me and now a new level of nostalgia emerges as she now reaches a milestone of crossing the threshold on graduation day.

To be honest, Mama, my heart breaks a little bit each time I am confronted with last moments but I need to keep reminding myself that the last moments lead to beautiful first moments ahead.

The first moment, with intense trepidation stepping foot on a college campus, the first moment meeting a new friend after years of being in the same friend group, or the first moment where she truly feels independent and thriving on her own as she now lives miles upon miles away from home for the first time.

Firsts are exhilarating while also dreadful.
Firsts are new paths forged while releasing the old.
Firsts are growing up while holding on.
Firsts often take our breath away from the anticipation and excitement but also from sheer fear.
Firsts can propel us forward but also hold us back trembling, not able to take another step.
Firsts bring about smiles of joy but also dread and anxiety.

Firsts mean opening up and trying new while wanting to stay right where we are.
Firsts mean taking the first step with faith and confidence.

I may want to hold tight to memory lane and revisit the precious moments of her childhood time and time again, but I also know doing this doesn't serve a purpose and is actually a disservice to her.

I need to allow her to launch to new heights and explore the many possibilities and firsts that are ahead of her.
I need to allow her to fail and pick herself back up and I need to allow her to keep striving forward without feeling a tug from behind holding her back.

So for now, my mama heart is soaking in all of the lasts of her senior year, while giving myself the grace to feel it all.
I may be watching a countless amount of old home videos, with a tissue in hand, but my heart needs to feel this as hard as it is some days.

But you know what doesn't end, Mama?
Our kids needing us to be there.
Our kids wanting us to be near them.
Our kids craving our love.

This never wavers...

And you know what we get to look forward to as they get older?

Late night talks in the kitchen.

Explosions of joy as college acceptance emails are opened and tears are combined with a deep exhale after a year of intense work.

Listening to views on faith and our world and so much more.

So as I grow alongside of my girl and she arrives home, with keys in hand, plops down at the island in the kitchen, and talks nonstop until the wee hours of the night, a core memory reminds me of the many nights I spent rocking her in the dark holding on and loving every cell of her being.

I'm reminded of the countless nights quietly spent singing a soft tune, as pudgy fingers met my lips and our gaze was only on each other.

This may be the hardest point in my motherhood journey thus far, but with a lump in my throat and tears cascading down my cheeks I am mustering up the courage, from deep within, to be the mom my daughter needs me to be. A mom celebrating each milestone and relishing in the many lasts while looking ahead with excitement and a sparkle in my eye for her future and cheering her on one step at a time as she encounters all of the exhilarating firsts, just as I did that early foggy morning as she tentatively stepped foot on the big yellow bus for her very first day of school.

Today I'm shifting my perspective and focusing on how all of the magical first moments help to shape my teen into who they are seeking to become and how blessed I am to witness this growth.

Reflection

A few lasts that are tugging at my heartstrings...
And
A few firsts that I'm excited about for my teen...

How Is Today Already Here?

College?
Wasn't it just the first day of preschool drop off as she giggled with excitement as a tear also trickled down her cheek?
Wasn't it just the first day of middle school where finding the perfect outfit was on the top of her list? And her nerves took over as she quietly walked out of the door?
Time...
It doesn't slow down for anyone as much as we desperately try to hold on.
Time is forever moving forward, guiding all of us and reminding us daily to hold on tight but still go along for the ride and not fight it.
How was I just holding this sweet girl, right after being born, still connected to me, and now she will be living on her own?
How was I just rocking her quietly to sleep singing lullabies and soon she will be tucking herself in each night?
How was I just tying her shoes that repeatedly wouldn't stay tied and now I'm looking eye to eye at a beautiful woman who now borrows my shoes?
But this girl here, she has some decisions to make...
tough decisions...
The hardest decision she has been faced with...
and we all know that decisions aren't easy.

Decisions...sometimes suck the life out of you.
Decisions...open you up to thoughts you didn't know you had.
Decisions...make you grow.
My girl is strong willed and perseverant while maintaining a kind heart.
She knows what she wants, who she wants to draw into her life and the kind of life she can see herself carry with pride.
But at the same time, she doesn't know.
Her mind is racing and she is trying to quiet her beating heart down a bit.
The excitement is rushing but she knows it is important to remain calm and not let impulsivity take over.
And I just watch with wonder.

I watch with pride...
So as I gaze at her, a deep joy enters my soul.
A peace washes over me.

Time may move on and we will both continue to grow but our hearts will always be intertwined...peace washes over me.

And just as we were connected so long ago, a cut of a cord or a new phase of life, does not mean a loss of a connection...peace washes over me.

Maybe now, the deeper, richer and more fulfilling connections begin... peace washes over me.

A new phase is about to begin...
peace washes over me.

The idea of my teen leaving home may be daunting but leaving the nest doesn't mean never returning home. It doesn't mean losing connection and it doesn't mean saying goodbye forever. It simply means an opportunity for growth and a deepening of the relationship that is to come.

Reflection

Ways I'm offering myself peace and encouragement during this new chapter...

Is My Heart Ready?

Is my heart ready?
Is she ready?
I know she's ready.
I knew this day was approaching. I knew the tough decision of choosing which college she would call home for the next four years was right around the corner, and I knew within seconds she would accept her enrollment to the college of her dreams by clicking one button on her laptop as she sat at the kitchen island emanating with joy.
My heart is beaming with pride as excitement emanates out of my pores.
But I can't deny it, there is also a twinge of self-doubt.
I know, it's silly.
But I can't push it away.
I can't pretend it isn't consuming my thoughts.
My mind is racing as my heart is pumping and questions are swirling around me catapulting me into a frenzy of thought bubbles floating over my head.
Did I teach her enough about life?
Does she feel strong knowing she has an armor of tools following with her? And does she know deep within her soul she can reach out at any time and I'll always be there?
Did I show her enough love?
Did I allow her to feel the rich emotions I feel for her?
Because sometimes it is hard to explain.

Sometimes life gets in the way.
Sometimes emotions and words are hard for me to communicate.
Will she close this door confidently knowing she is loved and will forever be loved?
I hope and pray this will be true.
Did I tell her and show her over and over again that she is enough? Just as she is?
Nothing more.
Nothing less.
Just her beautiful self for the world to be adorned with?
Will she walk with her head held high and be reminded she is enough and never question it?
Did I tell her and show her enough how proud I am?
Oh, I hope so.
Because this girl of mine allows my heart to swell with pride.
Her compassionate old soul captures hearts with pure kindness and there is nothing more she ever needs to do in life to make my heart beam with pride.
Sweet girl of mine, you are loved beyond measure and I silently pray your soul will carry my love with you always, as you embark on your new journey.

> *A mother is never prepared for letting go and the loss that she feels as her child grows up, just as she isn't prepared to step foot on the path of finding herself again. But here she is, ready to take flight, eagerly wondering who she is now and where this new journey will take her.*

Reflection

Questions I ponder as my teen grows up. . .

The Nest

Just as a Robin Red Breast builds her nest each spring to host her baby birds with devotion, compassion, and resilience, mothers do the same. It's a mirror image of our motherhood journey and a beautiful journey to witness in the making.

It's a mother creating space, a safe haven with sticks and materials that don't always match, yet creating a breathtaking masterpiece to provide comfort, support, and endless amounts of love within a home. And just like the Robin Red Breast, as mothers, we are always gathering, creating, and always attempting to make sure our homes are comfortable and as safe as possible.

We create a soft landing space for our "little birds" knowing we will make mistakes, have challenging days, and recognize with grace that being a mother isn't always easy but we are growing and learning as we travel this journey beside them.

We encourage through hardships.
We cheer for proud moments.
We love through it all.

Mothers are the providers of hope and givers of love.
We are needed both physically and emotionally, just like the mother bird, until the day comes where it's time to leave the nest.

A day that often brings about feelings of dread and anticipation, a day full of reflection and sadness. A day filled with more emotions than one even knows.

But just as the mother bird has to trust she has done everything possible leading up to this moment of flight to be a success, mamas do the same.

We work hard year after year, wondering if we have done enough, offered enough, loved enough. Did we give enough guidance about how to weather the storms to prepare for this very moment to soar on a journey that will take them far and fill their hearts with joy?

Mothers know leaving this curated nest may not be easy.
Our birds will falter.
They will fail and they will fall.
But they will continue to soar and move on.

And just as our nest empties out, we too need to accept the new journey before us, as moms.
We will falter.
We will fail and we will fall.
But we will continue to soar and move on.

Our nests may look different now, leaving us with a void that we feel in the depths of our souls. Maybe we don't feel needed or wanted anymore. Maybe we feel forgotten about or misplaced, or maybe we feel lost.

But within the emptiness there is also space for a subtle excitement for change and new beginnings to happen.

There is acceptance that a beautiful new chapter awaits and there are many breathtaking opportunities to embark on.

And just as the mother bird flies back-and-forth looking out for her nest and what rests inside, mamas continue to do the same. We are never far, always checking in, and attempting to continuously create connections.

So as the silence takes over, let's embrace the newness, wrap our arms around the stillness, and allow ourselves to hold tight to the old nest while cherishing the beauty within as we offer ourselves permission to also fly.

Leaving the nest doesn't mean never coming home.
This will always be home.
There will always be a nest where a mother loves hard and then she loves some more.

> *As new beginnings await me, I need to leave the heartache behind. I need to allow myself the gift of moving forward during this season of life even if it hurts to the core some days and look toward a future where I embark on all of the adventures ahead.*

Reflection

Ways my nest has changed and how I feel about it. . .

Missing You

As the summer begins, one chapter is coming to an end and a season of new beginnings are emerging for my daughter. As our teens embark on a journey taking them to college, the military, trade school, or a gap year, I always find that I'm at a loss for words. For me, I'm filled with excitement while also having a lump in my throat and a feeling of time passing by.

I'm going to miss my daughter once she leaves for college. I can't hide it. It doesn't take away my excitement for her, and I don't make her feel guilty about leaving, but it's a feeling I need to acknowledge and feel at this very moment, and that's okay.

Those late-night talks, as she tiptoes in, to let me know she's home, and then goes on and on about the evening, as I'm half-awake propped up on my pillow to focus on every word. . .
I'm going to miss this.

The messy room filled to the brim with water bottles and bowls, chocolate wrappers and make-up wipes on the floor. . .
I'm going to miss this (well maybe not all of the mess).

Her sweet laughter booming through the house as she and her friends swap stories over Mac and Cheese squeezing around the kitchen island. . .

Missing You

I'm going to miss this.

The daily morning wake up, since she hits snooze eight times and is still not awake...
I'm going to miss this.

Her warm embrace before she heads out of the door and a casual, "love you"...
I'm going to miss this.

The grace she shows her sisters when they are trying her last nerve by taking, yet again, a shirt without asking...
I'm going to miss this.

Her way with words as she tells a story about her dreams for the future, exaggerating at great length every fine detail of where her life will take her...
I'm going to miss this.

The mess of cornstarch and Buffalo sauce all over the floor late at night as she coats cauliflower for a much needed midnight snack...
I'm going to miss this.

Her shoes are in every corner of every room but yet none of them are hers...
I'm going to miss this.

The smell of nail polish wafting down the hallway as she screams with excitement on FaceTime...
I'm going to miss this.

The way she quietly asks if I'm okay after seeing I may not be. . . I'm going to miss this.

The countless dance performances and running all over town for new pointe shoes and sewing ribbons until my fingers bleed and ache. . .
I'm going to miss this.

Her silly demeanor, which simply shifts the tune in the house to laughter, as soon as she walks through the door. . .
I'm going to miss this.

Her never-ending desire to never empty the dishwasher. . .
I'm going to miss, or will I?

Her presence. . .just her. Her physical body being in the same room, talking on the couch before diving into the latest reality show, her warmth and love and zest for life. I'm just going to miss her. My girl! My daughter.

As moms, we are also transitioning and feeling a ton of emotions right now. It's not just our graduates who are embarking on a new journey, we are as well. We have created a family, raised our kids, and now we have to find our way while getting used to not seeing our kids daily. We are used to having daily face-to-face conversation and knowing the ins and outs of their daily life and now that chapter will come to a close.
But as a mom, who will go through this transition for the fourth time, I promise you this. . .the initial sadness will be replaced with pure happiness as you watch your child thrive.
Will you still miss them? Of course!
But will the transition become easier? Yes!

The greatest gift I can give my child is the ability to let them go in order to grow and thrive on their own.
This is the love of a mother.

Reflection

Things that have changed day to day and how I'm coping...

It's Hard to Let Go

Why are some days so much harder to let go?
Why do I remember each and every giggle, subtle whimper, and full-blown tantrum?
Why do I hold so tightly onto the toothless grin staring up at me and a little hand holding on to mine as we crossed the street, walked through the park, or snuggled on the couch?
Why do I yearn for the days of pushing the swing, hearing a sweet high-pitched voice begging to touch the sky one more time?

Mama, I don't necessarily yearn to go back to when my kids were younger but I wish I slowed down a bit to cherish the moment that we were in during that time.
I wish I didn't focus on an email, a phone call, or the text that was coming in.
I wish I wasn't so focused on sticking to the schedule of bath time and bedtime, what to make for dinner, and I wish I didn't pay attention to what activity to sign up for and if the neighbor's kids were going to camp.
I wish I just lived in the moment.

So here I am now, a mom raising teens and young adults, and all I wish is to go back to truly living in the moment. But you see, Mama. I can't.
All I can do is change today and move forward and attempt my best to live in the moment now with zero regrets.

I am making a promise to myself to embrace the stage of motherhood I am in and I look forward to witnessing the priceless gift of watching my grown kids evolve and flourish on their path of adulthood.

I am relishing who they are, the mistakes made and the multitude of lessons that are barreling their way that they will conquer.

I'm watching all of these moments unfold in front of my eyes, and all I can do is silently say a prayer for one of life's greatest blessings that touches my heart each day.

I'm not going to make the mistake of rushing through life and parenting, seeking something else, and having a desire to be somewhere else. I am going to sit tight, hold on, and gaze as the young adults before me become who they are meant to be and what a blessing this is to witness within this moment of time. A time I will cherish from where I am now.

A heavy heart during this season of motherhood brings about a lot of emotions. Our kids leaving home brings about a sense of loss and grief but it can also bring about a profound sense of growth for us moms.

Reflection

A few things I'm having a hard time letting go of and why...

I'm Trying

It's hard letting you go a little bit more, day by day, but be patient with me through this process...
I'm trying.
It's hard watching you continue to grow, knowing in the near future you will be on your own...
I'm trying.
It's hard reliving memories and often wanting to put it all on pause...
I'm trying.
It's hard knowing I have made so many mistakes and wish I could go back in time and redo it all...
I'm trying.
It's hard believing my child with dirty knees wishing for one more "under dog" is now ready to put on a cap and gown and fly...
I'm trying.
It's hard gazing at you, feeling flooded with hundreds of emotions and attempting to keep it all together...
I'm trying, so please be patient with me.
But you know what isn't hard?
It's not hard watching you overcome challenges, persevere, and find your path.
It's not hard embracing every moment you feel joy and allowing it to seep inside of me too.

I'm Trying

It's not hard to listen to your laugh, the same laugh you had as a toddler.
It's not hard to know, even though miles will soon separate us, you are ready to be on your own. You are independent with a strong head on your shoulders.
It's not hard to relish in your accomplishments for each one is well deserved.
It's not hard to embrace you and feel all of our hugs since the beginning of time.
It's not hard to gaze at you with wonder, as tears form and a smile takes over, for I know your future is nothing but bright.
It's not hard to watch you love.
It's not hard to watch you live.
It's not hard to watch you grow into your authentic self.
It's not hard to watch you share your gifts with the world.
As I stand by watching you, please be patient. Because even though I am watching a miraculous blessing grow in front of my eyes, it's hard some days.
But know I'm trying...
I'm trying to let go bit by bit to fully allow your wings to slowly open and soar...
Soar to depths you only know.
So as you continue to fly along your journey, in your heart of hearts please know, I am trying...
and this mama will continue to send you silent prayers of comfort, love, and all you have ever dreamed of for your beautiful, magical life.

My grown child flying on their own isn't a threat to me as a mom or our relationship. Rather, it validates that I have prepared them to take on the world.

Reflection

Life has changed throughout this letting go season, and it hasn't always been easy. A few ways life has been hard. . .

Always a Mom

Our job isn't over when our big kids head to college or wherever else their path leads them.
Our job as a mom continues to live on inside of them and deep inside of ourselves as the woman who knows every inch of their soul.
But for some reason, we are told otherwise. We read repeatedly false messages that scare mothers to believe that our relationship with our kids are severed once they turn 18 and our connection becomes void.

Mama, please don't fall into the trap of these false lies.
Being a mom never ends.
Our spirits live on within them long after we even take our last breath, so hold on tight to that hope knowing your role as a mom is forever embedded in their heart.

No matter how many miles separate us from our big kids or even if they live at home, they need us.
Our kids still need us.
They will continue to reach out to us with questions about their favorite childhood recipe or how to get a stain out of their favorite shirt.

They need us to answer calls when they need to vent, seeking our validation as well as moments to share good news about internships and job opportunities, people they have met, who they fall in love with, and even how to make our families famous grilled cheese sandwich to perfection.

They need to know they can still fall into our arms when life takes a turn and that the road to home is always accessible and filled with insurmountable amounts of love, comfort, and their favorite snacks.

They need to still know we have their back supporting them through every dip and challenge as well as the multitude of celebrations that will come their way. They need to know they are valued and loved and most importantly adored for who they are as their unique and authentic self.

So Mama, don't fall for the trap that our time as a mom is up just because our kids are grown up and living out of the safe haven of our homes.
Being a mom is far from over.
Actually, it's just the beginning as this new chapter of life unfolds before our eyes for both our kids and ourselves and what a gift to walk this journey together side by side.

Our big kids need us.

Our job as a mom doesn't come to an end and the title of mom never leaves us but naturally our role needs to change. For us to be the mom our grown kid needs, we must adapt and adjust to who they need us to be for them now.

Reflection

My role as a mom is changing and a few examples of how. . .

Packed Bags

Hang in there, Mama
my own words echo, as I'm about to embark on the bittersweet moment of college drop off.

Hang in there, Mama...
as we gather around our family table, laughing while choking back tears and filling our bellies to fill a void.

Hang in there, Mama...
as the last load of laundry is folded and placed in bags.

Hang in there, Mama...
as her room slowly empties out and only the hollowed memories of childhood remain.

Hang in there, Mama...
as friends come in and out, for one last bit of laughter, to swell their hearts and carry them through, until they see each other again.

Hang in there, Mama...
as bags are lining the hallway reminding me this is truly happening and to take a deep breath.

Hang in there, Mama...
daily life will be different but keep this friendly reminder close by...the love established will remain a constant.

Hang in there, Mama...
as the memory bank of my little girl with pigtails and sparkly shoes takes over.

Hang in there, Mama...
as the independent, grown woman in front of me zips up any last minute items before heading out the door ready to conquer the world.

Hang in there, Mama...
as I quietly savor her smile, which says it all...

She will be okay.
She is ready.
She is beyond prepared.
She is going to make a difference.
She is independent and strong and balanced and true to herself.
She is all I hope to be.

Hang in there, Mama...
as elation outweighs the sadness, for her joy fills my cup up and overflows each day.

Hang in there, Mama...
as my arms wrap around my sweet child, one more time, gently letting go, knowing this isn't goodbye while allowing my heart to crumble a little bit.
So as my throat tightens, as I give one last hug, may the words, Hang in There, Mama keeps me grounded as tears roll from my eyes.

Raising my children while loving and supporting them isn't the difficult part. The hard part is letting them go when all I really want is for them to stay here forever in my arms.

Reflection

I offer myself support during moments of sadness when I...

Goodbyes Are Hard

As the heavy steel door of the expansive brick dorm locks behind me, it takes my breath away. The days and weeks leading up to this goodbye have held a tight grip on my heart. A grip I'm embarrassed to say is more of an ache. An ache that runs deep and a feeling that wraps around my throat suffocating me to the point that I no longer have words. And I can only imagine that so many of you are feeling this ache as well and feeling a bit suffocated by this moment in time.

But Mama, even though the emotions encompassing my heart may last a bit longer than I would like, I'm not going to push these intense feelings aside and ignore it.
I'm going to embrace each emotion as it comes just as I also have to accept the locked door closing behind me.
The locked door and my emotions carry the same weight. Just as I can't re-enter the dorm unless my girl buzzes me in with permission, I also have to allow myself the permission to feel.
To feel the weight of her childhood slipping through my fingers.
To feel the weight of letting go.
To feel the weight of holding on but setting up healthy boundaries.
And to feel the weight of motherhood slowly changing before me.

I have to come to the realization though that the lock on the door may not allow me into the narrow hallways of the dorm, but it doesn't mean I'm locked out of her heart, her life, or big dreams. This is the truth about our kids growing up. Our time being a mom doesn't end, it evolves. It changes with each passing day and our role is different, but it doesn't end and we aren't locked out forever. We just now need to ask for permission to be entered in while respecting our now grown kids' decision.

And with a bang, as the steel meets the newly minted lock, my heart steps back in time...

Back to a little key resting on top of her childhood bedroom door for the "just in case moment," where she by accident locked herself in the room and I needed to rescue her.

Back when the side door of our home was faithfully unlocked so she and her friends could travel in and out carelessly to grab some grapes, kick off their muddy shoes, and find a moment at home to exhale and rest.

Back to the day when she was gently placed in my loving arms and she unlocked a piece of my heart that had been aching and yearning for stillness and love. And in that very moment I began to truly live because her grace changed my heart forever.

There are so many moments forever embedded and locked within this nostalgic heart of mine as I stand outside the dorm room door, heart pounding, not wanting to say goodbye. But as I gently rub her head, as we hug one last time, I'm comforted in knowing this girl will never be locked out of my home or my heart.

She may live miles upon miles away from home now, but the road leading home will always carry the love of her childhood and a side door unlocked waiting for her to return as her gentle voice says, "Mom, I'm home."

Before I became a mother I never knew how my children would soothe my soul and be the healing agent I so desperately needed as I continued along my lifelong journey of being a mom.

Reflection

A nostalgic moment reflecting on my children's childhood that captures my heart and takes my breath away...

The Changing Season

It hit me today. This season of my life is almost done.
The season that I've been holding onto for so long, not wanting anything to change, and it's almost coming to an end. Some days I feel like I'm suffocating, barely able to breathe or gather enough air to fill up my lungs.

I hate goodbyes.
I don't like endings.
I despise change.

Our bustling home once filled to the brim with lots of people and an abundant amount of love is changing as everyone is beginning to embark on their own journeys and for some reason this suddenly hit me today as I was driving on a busy highway with cars whizzing past me. As tears streamed down my face, I was taken off guard and reminded of this brutal reality. It's a truth I have been avoiding, but today my body stopped pretending and ignoring and felt, for the first time in months, the ache I had so desperately been pushing aside.

Continuing to drive with tears rolling down my cheeks and reddening my green eyes torturing myself listening to Taylor Swift's "Never Grow Up," I was starkly reminded of how numb I truly have become pretending this moment wasn't going to one day arrive.

The Changing Season

Why would I keep pushing aside the truth?
Why couldn't I accept that my motherhood journey was about to change?
Why couldn't I simply allow myself to face the reality of my kids growing up and moving on?

Change scares me.
But what if rather than fighting this transitional time of my kids growing older, I soaked it all in and embraced it?

Embrace the change.
Embrace the difference.
Embrace what's ahead.

It doesn't eliminate my hesitation but rather shifts the perspective and allows me space to willingly let go of my emerging young adults before me and let them fly.

Mama, it's hard.
Some days I ignore it, maybe you do the same, and other days I'm an open wound, oozing with emotion, needing to be taken care of, comforted, and soothed.

But today it really hit me.

You see, Mama, I have a new season beginning and I'm scared.
Will I be happy?
Do I even know who I am anymore?
Who am I without my kids being here?

And as the cars drove past me today, speeding by one by one, I thought about my motherhood journey throughout the past 21 years.

Just as the cars drive by, some of them know exactly where they are going and exactly where the journey takes them and the destination ahead, while other cars casually drive miles upon miles hoping to find a beautiful place to stop along the way, and this right there is where my heart is in this moment.

Some days I feel numb about what's lost.
Some days I feel dizzy with excitement about what's ahead.
Some days I have no idea where I'm going and hoping to find joy in the journey and some days I am confident in the direction I'm going.

And it's okay if you feel this way too, Mama.
This season is new.
This season is scary sometimes.
This season is going to be a new journey for all of us.

Hang in there, Mama.
You've got this!

Prioritizing myself after years of raising kids is not selfish. It is essential to learn who I am today and finally embrace myself with all of the self-love I deserve.

Reflection

My honest thoughts on what change really feels like for me right now. . .

Worn Out Shoes

As I stare at my daughter's worn-out, tattered, and stained shoes near the door, I can't bear the thought of putting them away. She recently left for college, and my heart isn't yet ready to accept all of the little changes to our house, and somehow leaving her shoes there continues to make our house feel like home. It's a little reminder that she is always a part of me and home isn't forgotten about even as she travels on to this new chapter of her life.

Her shoes carried her through the trials of high school, the first party she attended, the many football games in the rain, the walks in the neighborhood to visit a childhood friend, and so much more. Her shoes are a reminder of her childhood but also a reminder of the beautiful journey and road she is navigating now. I may not be with her and her old shoes may have been left behind, but her shoes by the door continue to remind me of walking through life with her.

Maybe it's silly, Mama, but I hope when she walks through the door again, after many hours flying home, her eyes see her shoes still placed exactly where they were left when she said goodbye and she feels a sense of peace knowing a little part of her was always home even though she was miles away. I hope she knows that home will always be waiting for her return with an open door and her shoes nearby.

Because you see, Mama, I think a mother, with open arms waiting to embrace her child is no different than the shoes she puts on her feet each and every day. We both offer support and to take on the weight she may be transporting around yet at the end of the day we both offer relief as she slips the shoes off and steps barefoot on the floor of her home which offers love, support, and a time to exhale.

Mothers, like the soles of shoes, both keep moving forward and encouraging step by step even on the days it's hard to put one foot in front of the other. The shoes may become worn, torn, and tattered but just like a mother, a perfect pair of shoes doesn't exist. So as she travels the many pathways of life, leaving her worn out shoes behind at home may she always know both her shoes and her mom are waiting to offer support as she travels the road ahead. Just as the shoes travel the miles, a mother's love stretches the distance of time.

But unlike the tattered shoes she will one day outgrow and throw away, her mother's love is irreplaceable and will always remain.

A mother's love never changes. It's a love that is unconditional from the beginning of time and will never waver. A mother's love is felt yesterday, today, and for all of the tomorrows.

Reflection

A few ways I express unconditional love to my children. . .

Crying Over a Car

I cried today over a car.
Mama, have you ever cried as you let go of something that you didn't even know held so much value or purpose? Have your tears ever flowed so quickly you couldn't quite grasp what was going on and you were washed away in a sea of emotion?

Well, today I cried as I traded in my car which for so long defined me as a mom.
I cried today as I let go of so many memories.

I cried today, remembering the curdled milk sippy cups, found under the seat of the car weeks later, the French fries smashed into the floor, playing Bucky Beaver but putting an end to the game because the punching got out of hand.

I cried today as I reminisced about the numerous carpools to and from volleyball, the back-and-forth driving to dance lessons, and changing in the car to get there on time while eating a snack.
I cried today thinking about all of the Christmas Eves the six of us drove over to Nana and Poppy's house, numerous ski trips with the trunk filled to the brim with luggage, and everyday trips to the store.

I cried today, remembering all of the times my girls were lulled to sleep in this car whether it was out of pure exhaustion, a tantrum when they were toddlers, or sometimes just the stress of life as the teen years began.
I cried today, remembering how many times I've sat waiting in this car. Waiting to pick up from school and orthodontist appointments, or waiting at sporting events or outside of a late night party.

I cried today thinking of how many phases of motherhood I have traveled within this car.
I cried today thinking about how much I have changed throughout my motherhood journey and how many secrets and prayers the walls of this car have heard.
I cried today knowing a new chapter of my life is beginning. A chapter where all of my children will soon be off on their own.
I cried today as pieces of their childhood are left behind, nostalgia takes over, and the new journey of becoming an empty nester begins.
I cried today for the past, but I also know there is a beautiful future ahead.
I cried today, knowing our family has been connected beyond measure through this car, but also knowing that we will forever remain connected.

I cried today and guess what, Mama, it's okay if you did too, because that's what being a mom is about.
It's crying for the past, embracing the present, and moving forward to the future, while feeling blessed for the simple moments, as a family growing up together.
I cried today.

Letting go doesn't begin as our child gets older. As moms, we have been preparing ourselves all along and letting go throughout each stage of watching our child grow up. This right here is motherhood.

Reflection

A material possession that has sentimental value to me and why...

My end goal as a mom is for my grown children to choose to spend time with me.

I'm Scared. . .

Can I tell you a secret?
Some days I am absolutely terrified to become an empty nester.

Please, Mama, don't get me wrong. I'm thrilled my kids are where they're meant to be as they move on to college and beyond. But it doesn't mean I'm not scared.

Mama, to be honest though, I'm not scared for them, I'm scared for who I am and who I have become while raising my kids and I think it's something we don't talk about enough.

We don't talk about this huge looming transition that hangs over a mother's head, knowing their last one is leaving the comfort of home.

I know that leaving the nest doesn't imply never coming home again and it doesn't mean connections are severed, but I think I'm scared of what is to come for me.

Who am I anymore?
Did I get lost along the way as I raised my kids?
Did I forget about my passions and what makes me my unique self?

I am scared.
I haven't been alone for years.

My husband and I haven't spent much time together without the distraction of kids for years.

Are we going to embrace this change as a union supporting each other?

Is our marriage going to pull through this?

Have we invested enough time in our marriage throughout the years of raising our children to go back to one another and still be in love or are we going to be lonely and bored not knowing what to do?

So as I get ready for my daughter to leave, my last one out the door, I can't help but be a little nervous, and I surely can't help but be scared.

I can't help but have some overwhelming anxiety taking over and waking me up in the middle of the night.

What I know though is this: I can't be the only one feeling this way. I'm not the only one who is so excited for my child to read an acceptance email from a college, but at the same time breaking apart inside with the fear of not knowing what I am going to do once my big kid leaves.

And guess what, it doesn't make me selfish for thinking these thoughts. It means I am human and have feelings that I didn't know existed within my body until a few short months ago.

But I am hopeful that with time I am going to find that place of being comfortable with the new stage of parenting that I am in.

And I know that with each passing day I am going to gain confidence and I'm going to stop questioning because the truth is, I will be okay.

I'm Scared...

I will be okay because I am more than just a mom.

I am a woman with so much more life to live and Mama, on those days self-doubt creeps in for you surrounding this new empty nesting phase please know, we are all trying to figure it out together but also remember there is always beauty in the hope of tomorrow.

Even though I may be sad or scared of this new chapter of my life I am making a promise to myself. A promise to live authentically and embrace the breathtaking moments ahead rather than getting sucked down in the trap of denial.

Reflection

A few things I'm scared of as I enter the empty nesting season...

Luggage and Letting Go

As my college kid begins to pack her bags, I know once again it's time for a goodbye, and I'm not so good at goodbyes.
Goodbyes take a toll on me, make me uneasy to the point of nausea, and cause me to retreat and become quiet. But as I see the hard plastic luggage and packing cubes come out of the closet, I prepare myself for what's to come.

It's time for my heart to break a bit and ache a little.
It's time for my heart to also spend a few days healing. Healing from the wounds of our goodbye, yet knowing that letting go is essential for her well-being.

As she sets out on her new journey and puts in her bags little particles of her life, old memories mixed with new, there is nothing more that I could ever want for her, even as the ache begins to take over.

She is independent.
She is strong.
She is capable and fierce.

Luggage and Letting Go

She has a desire to be her authentic self, never backing down, while remaining emotionally connected.

I always knew as a mom that letting go was inevitable, but what I didn't know is that it would hurt this much. But, if I have learned one thing as mom, it's that we have to let go of our kids in order for them to grow, just as we have to let go in order for them to learn.

We have to let go in order for our kids to create and follow their dreams while navigating through the path of the unknown and what's ahead.

So as little items are put in the bag, with friendly reminders of things not to forget, my heart does ache, yet it's full of life and happiness at the same time recalling the precious memories of her childhood.

As I help with the final touches and zip up her bag, a little bit of pink creeps out.

It's a pink that I know so well after years of hugging, loving, and handwashing.

It's a pink that has aged over the years, changed over time, lost its color and fluff, but a pink that has and always will be a constant in her life.

My girl may be old enough to travel and explore the world, but she is not yet ready to let go of her pink piggy, her comfort and her best childhood friend.

So as I see shades of her pinkish gray favorite stuffed animal, peeking out of her carry-on bag, I softly smile and silently exhale knowing her childhood was filled with love and the many comforts of home.

Being a mother is complicated. It's yearning for alone time to gather yourself together and regroup, yet the moment your child walks out of the door you miss them terribly. Motherhood is humbling like that and forever will be.

Reflection

My thoughts on goodbyes...

Staying Strong

Whoosh!

And just like that anxiety came back, and boy did it arrive like a beast.

She knows she's strong.
She knows she can balance the new emerging journey and all of the junk thoughts entering her mind. She knows it won't last forever.

But anxiety tends to do that. It plays brutal tricks on us and makes us feel in control and then – whoosh – the next second feeling scared to death, barely breathing, and not sure how to handle the day-to-day basics of a new university, making friends, and being away from the comfort of home.

But, oh, my mama heart... she wasn't expecting this, so there are a whole lot of tears, and I'm not shying away from my tears.
My tears are filled with empathy.
My tears are filled with self-doubt.
Did I not help her enough and guide her enough to get the help needed to conquer this challenge?
Maybe you feel something similar to this as well during this stage of motherhood.

Anxiety. . .it's a beast.

But you know it's interesting about anxiety?
We know in due time she will once again be able to breathe without a cold shower poring over her body, or ice packs for her wrist and neck, and without needing to write down every thought that is a fact rather than a worry.

We know that she will get through this. We know she is resilient and we know the tools and strategies she needs to carry her through to a lifetime of fulfillment and happiness, but today anxiety is a beast that is taking over.

It is making her feel sick, have a loss of appetite, and simply not like herself. She feels trampled by her thoughts, consumed in her worry, ruminating, and wondering what comes next. How do I handle this, and will it last forever?

She is silent behind her tears. She is overwhelmed with sadness and grief from leaving home yet knows she has a beautiful opportunity in front of her and is trying her best to embrace it, but anxiety is a beast taking hold of her.

She is struggling pushing forward. She feels like she is drowning trying to meet new people and make lifelong friends. She is walking to classes, with trepidation, but still going. Anxiety is a beast.

But with each new day she knows she will continue to take one step forward and put one foot in front of the other. She is conquering this battle as she embarks on her new journey. A journey she will not allow her anxiety to take over. But my mama heart feels this to my core.

Anxiety is a beast.

There is nothing more powerful than witnessing your child's strength and tenacity. There will be times of hardship and turmoil, but through it all they will become the person they always dreamed of becoming and what a gift to watch.

Reflection

When anxiety or worry takes over, a few tools I use to get me thorough...
Or a few tools I use to help my teen through their anxiety...

One of Those Moms

I'm one of those moms now...

who gazes a little longer while they walk past a new mom holding a baby and who can't stop smiling as I watch a tired mom navigate the grocery store with kids hanging onto the cart and climbing all over her.

I'm one of those moms now...

who stares and smiles and probably talks for too long to anyone she meets, who relishes in the future, while still holding onto the past ever so tightly.

I'm one of those moms now...

who gushes while looking at a baby's chubby fingers and toes and remembers with fine detail every inch of my child, who has nostalgia rush back and trample over my body, while laughter, joy, and sadness bring me back to old moments in time.

I'm one of those moms now...

who can't stop taking photos, knowing how important they are down the road while also attempting to live in the moment to not miss it all, who is considered an old-timer in the neighborhood, and as I drive by all of the moms, with toddlers in strollers meeting on the corner for a morning walk, all I can do is wave and remember.

I'm one of those moms now...

who drives past the park and can recall vivid memories of climbing on the monkey bars, and searching through goopy muck for frogs, but now eats sushi for lunch rather than the leftover pieces of a cream cheese and jelly sandwich or bits of chicken nuggets.

I'm one of those moms now...

who wishes to go back in time but also is eager to see what the future holds.

I'm one of those moms now...

but I am also the same mom who will forever recall the moment my sweet babies were placed in my arms, because that is truly the moment my life began.

I will always and forever be that mom.

> *I'm the mom who's nostalgic. It's who I am, and I'm proud of that. I will always take photos, save little notes, and attempt to capture family moments.*
> *It's who I am.*

Reflection

Ways I can relate to being one of those moms now...

From Heartache to Happiness

Some say it will get easier each time I watch my girl's luggage disappear from me and closer to her departure gate, but I'm not so sure.

Who knew my heart would ache, yet again, as she walked away?

Who knew as the day drew closer to her departure my throat would constrict and my heart would race faster?

Who knew hugging her each day, multiple times a day, would cause an ease to wash over me and soothe my soul?

But one thing I know is her happiness takes away some of my ache.

Who knew months ago, her rich growth and development of self would be astounding to witness?

Who knew memories would become ones she holds so dear?

Who knew layers and layers would peel away as she learns more about who she truly is while becoming her true self?

From Heartache to Happiness

But one thing I know is her happiness takes away some of my ache.

Who knew listening to stories about her new lifelong friends would fill me up?

Who knew watching a sparkle fill her eyes, while talking about classes, goals, and experiences would fill me up with a dose of ecstatic enthusiasm?

Who knew gazing at the blooming adult standing before me would take my breath away then fill up my lungs with gratitude?

But one thing I know is her happiness takes away some of my ache.

So as I help zip up her luggage, I'll say a prayer of thanks for the little moments.

It's not easy letting go again but maybe one day it will get a bit easier.

But for now, I'm okay right where I am, walking away with tears in my eyes, as I hold tightly to all of the love I have in my heart for my sweet child.

The adult walking away, with luggage in hand, is still the same girl who once held my hand throughout the airport as her bunny dangled in the other.

So as she embarks down the long corridor of the airport, now alone, to the massive world awaiting her, I take a deep breath knowing she will forever carry a piece of my heart wherever her path may lead, and for that I am blessed.

I never knew that being a mother would tug at my heartstrings as much as it does. I never knew my heart would break so many times, and I never knew the joy that would enter my soul and fill me up. Being a mother may not be for the faint of heart, but I wouldn't trade it for anything in the world.

Reflection

A few ways my heartache becomes happiness. . .

Home

My daughter called me today from college, and she said something so simple.
My heart melted as the words she spoke held so much kindness and honesty.
She recalled one of those simple moments when she lived at home. She said, "Mom, I never thought I would miss home as much as I do right now."

Mama, right there, in that moment, I realized that all of those times where self-doubt took over and the hours upon hours I spent worrying if I was doing the right thing as a mom, came to a screeching halt, and right then and there I realized I did something right.

You see, one of my many goals as a mom is for my daughter to recall home where a sense of peace and calm takes over her heart. Our kids don't live at home forever, and those quiet moments where we open our hearts up and share our souls at the kitchen table are what they are going to remember with fondness.

She may not remember each and every conversation or joke that was told, but she is going to remember how the candle burned, balanced perfectly on a coaster with a photo of a bird's nest, as she shared her heart.

And one day, she is going to light a candle, as her kids sit sharing their dreams, and go back to her safe space of childhood.

She will go back to all of the moments she cherished as a way to go back in time and relive the memories of her childhood that made an imprint on her soul and the movie reel of her life.

My hope is for these memories to fill a part of her heart that will always remain a safe space where she can go back to at any moment and use it as a salve when her heart is weary and I have a feeling that you feel this way too, Sweet Mama.

Maybe it's recalling the fall day where we went on a hike to pick apples and the long drive home on the windy roads past the orchards smelling their sweet scent as the fresh air swept through the windows. Or maybe she can see us peeling the crisp red apples together, side by side, as the counter became covered in peels and the floury mixture of dough had just the right amount of sweetness with the perfect amount of cinnamon on top.

Maybe she is going to think back to all of our dance parties our home once held, as the walls echoed her favorite songs that soothed her soul and made her heart smile even on the days she felt her world was crumbling around her.

Maybe she will hear the cherished Johnny Mathis Christmas album I listened to as a child and get lost in it, as she takes out grandma's cherished Christmas plates to set the table just as she did as a little girl making sure each place setting was set with love.

So as I gaze out of the window, into the backyard she once skipped around collecting acorns and fireflies, I am reminded of the fact that many miles separate us as she now sits in her dorm room. A space she has created and made as cozy as possible, but it will never be home. It's not a space that wraps her up in a hug and breathes new life into her when she feels empty. It's a temporary home for now as she waits for her next flight home to be embraced by the arms of her loved ones and the home that knows every little secret she has in her heart.

A peaceful home where whether big or small doesn't matter and a fresh coat of paint or walls chipping away means nothing. What matters is a home filled with countless blessings, unconditional love, and peace filling up the air so as she walks through the door she can finally exhale and breathe new life, filled with love, back up into every cell of her body and say, "It's good to be home."

May my home be filled with the laughter of childhood memories and love seeping into every crevice of every corner. And may my grown children know that the road leading home is always open with loving arms waiting for their return.

Reflection

My vision of what I hope "home" means to my children. . .

Broccoli

Who knew that picking out a head of broccoli in the grocery store one early afternoon could throw me over the edge.
I would've never imagined that this ordinary moment standing among the colorful produce under the fluorescent lights and being chilled by the refrigeration section would cause me to stop dead in my tracks. But, Mama, this simple act threw me for a loop, twirled me around where I couldn't see straight and left me barely standing and heavily breathing as tears welled up in my eyes.
Damn broccoli!

But here's the thing...it wasn't the broccoli; it was not knowing how much broccoli to purchase, and it completely caught me off guard. You see, I knew my house was emptying out when my youngest, twins, left for college, but never did I imagine that my emotions about empty nesting would lead me to this moment where time stood still. As I stared at the plethora of broccoli heads, sadness creeped in, and I finally realized all of the emotions surrounding my four daughters not living at home that I was storing deep inside of me and suppressing came rushing out. I was pushing all of the emotions I was feeling down into a cylinder within my gut, not paying attention to my thoughts until I came face-to-face with the broccoli. And boy, did we have a face off!

I came crashing down in that moment feeling alone, out of control, and questioning who I was. My identity and how I viewed myself was slowly being stripped away from me, and I was also faced with the harsh reality that I had to accept that my girls grew up and didn't live at home any longer. They moved on to the place where they are meant to be, and I needed to come to terms with it. I had to stop ignoring, and I had to grieve this loss of motherhood. I couldn't continue this way. Shoving my emotions down, not processing them, and pretending that they didn't exist wasn't healthy for anyone. I needed to face the truth, no matter how hard that was and accept that motherhood was different now.

My home was now quiet, my role as a mom changed a bit, and the amount of broccoli purchased needed to also change.

Standing there in the aisle alone I grabbed one small head of broccoli for two and with a heavy feeling weighing me down I mustered up a load of strength, gathered my composure, and wiped my tears away. As I took a deep breath, flashbacks of my girls all sitting at the dinner table, in the same seats they sat in night after night, came flooding back. The moments surrounding the countless evenings, around the table while sharing the highs and lows of our day, will forever remain close to my heart even when we are miles apart. But for now, I know one thing to be true, a mama's heart is tender just like perfectly cooked broccoli.

As I travel my motherhood journey, I have realized it's the little things. It's those small moments in time that capture my heart and take my breath away. It's the ordinary moments that make me take pause and fill up my emotional cup. It's the little things that remind me that being a mother is my greatest blessing.

Reflection

One thing that threw me over the edge on one of my first days home without my big kid. . .

A New Season

Mama,
Can I be honest with you?

This empty nesting season is a little rough, and it's seriously pulling at my heartstrings.
It's been two weeks since my four daughters left for college, and I'm waiting for the day I can walk down the hall toward the empty bedrooms. My heart is feeling an ache I have never experienced before. It's a dull pounding taking over my heart.

It's a bizarre feeling that is hard to explain, but I'm trying to move forward each day and begin to accept this new chapter of my life. I've known for a long time the house was going to empty out, but I wasn't expecting the intense feeling of emotions surrounding this moment, especially not being able to walk down the hallway to the bedrooms. I'm just hoping that with time, it becomes a little bit easier.

I'm blessed that my husband decided to pick up the rooms, strip the beds, and take care of throwing out the countless water bottles littering the rooms without even saying anything. I think he knew it was going to be too hard for me to enter the rooms and the memories that would come flooding back like a projector showcasing the very best moments of my life, but I'm hoping as we move forward I can see that there is new life for me in this season, as well as for my kids.

Mama, we are all adjusting within this empty nesting season. We are all figuring this out as we go, putting one foot in front of the other and moving forward, but it's hard. I can assure you that.

No one can say this is easy.
It's not easy.
It's one of the biggest challenges I've ever been faced with as a mother and a spouse.

Maybe it's because for the last 21 years of raising my children, with everyone living at home, my husband and I were rarely alone. Yet now we are faced with the reality that it's just the two of us, and we need to shift our perspective of what our home looks like.

It's looking forward to all of the new possibilities and opportunities that we have put on hold and look forward to revisiting our past and the things that we are passionate about doing together, while finding the joy in the simple quiet moments together again. It's not rushing around from place to place, scarfing dinner down our throats, just to make it to a game on time, but rather it's sitting and relishing in the peace and quiet.

But Mama, to be honest, some nights the peace and quiet is suffocating.
It's not something I'm used to.
I'm used to the side door being a gateway for kids going in and out, shoes all over the place, and dishes in the sink and sprawled all over the kitchen counter.

A New Season

I'm used to chaos and a vibrant bustling household.

But now, in this season, I have to learn to accept the quiet and find joy in this new chapter but it's not easy.

Many days are challenging, but I will admit the days are getting easier as time moves on.
It's not as difficult.
Mama, if you are struggling to embrace this new phase of your life just know that you are not alone. It's a challenging and difficult time for so many of us, but the sooner we embrace it and accept this new beginning, the sooner our hearts will heal.

> *As our teens get older letting go doesn't mean severing connections or abandoning them. Rather it means giving them the beautiful gift of responsibility and moving forward along their journey.*

Reflection

I'm embracing the empty nesting season or leading up to the season by...

What Do You Do?

What does a mom do when she sees her girl for the first time in six weeks?
She gasps as tears form in her eyes.

What does a mom do, to make every moment, within 48 hours count, so when she's home again her emotional cup is full?

She holds hand and talks and laughs and soaks in as much time as possible beside her.

She walks down the road, arms embraced, taking in every moment with her girl, now an adult taller and wiser than her.

She soaks it in, lets it settle, and holds each conversation close to her heart.

She embraces the silence and relishes in the simple chatter.

She holds close being introduced to friends, while hugging them tight, thanking them for taking care of her girl.

She listens, and listens some more, to the breathtaking stories of her girl finding her way while navigating her new journey.
She stares and gazes and can't help but have the movie reel of life start playing...

Isn't this the same girl who once snuggled me so close, night after night, for just one more kiss?

Isn't this the same girl who once asked me to rest each night, stroking her hair and singing lullabies, before finally closing her drowsy eyes?

Isn't this the same girl who once held my hand tightly and never let go until one day she did and I didn't know it was the last day?

Last days are hard...

So what does a mom do when it's the last day?

Whether it's the last day holding hands to cross the busy street before they do it on their own or the last day of a college visit, a mom has to do the same thing over and over again.

She has to hold on tight, while slowly letting go.

> *One of the hardest parts of being a mom is knowing that one day each moment becomes the last and we never know when that day will be.*

Reflection

Some things I miss from the younger years. . . .

The New Me

Since my youngest left for college I have been taking time to reflect and pause. I'm trying to decipher if I am happy that my house is quiet or if I am sad. What I do know is one part of my motherhood journey has come to an end and another one is beginning. I'm working on figuring it all out, but what I need to do is give myself time and grace to pause. I need to step back and think about the past, today, and what tomorrow holds.

But in the meantime, as I sit in my pause, I have decided now is the time to work on reconnecting with myself after many years. My identity for so long has been raising my four girls, and I quickly realized after dropping my youngest, twins, off at college that this process was not going to happen on its own. I needed to put in the dirty work and the emotional healing it entails, not busywork, not filling my time writing, and especially not filling my time hoping to find enough clothes lying around to put on a load of laundry, but offer myself time for reflection and meditation.

Life has changed and yes, the laundry is now done every few days rather than multiple times a day, and I'm embracing it. The dishwasher goes on once a day rather than two, and I'm embracing it. Crumbs don't litter the floor anymore, and I even see how

The New Me

shiny the floors are, which I have never noticed before, and I'm embracing it. I now go to bed earlier and wake up earlier, and I'm embracing it.

But Mama, I'm also embracing that it's okay to feel anxious about these changes and sad at times not knowing what's to come and missing what used to be.

It's okay to worry about my college kids and everything that goes along with them living away from home and it's okay to randomly start to well up in the car as a song comes on the radio reminding me of the countless drives where the open air was our therapy and soothed whatever was troubling our hearts. But most of all I'm trying my best to embrace the new season and the woman I'm allowing myself to be.

Sometimes I wonder though who is this woman that I am I becoming?
Can I stay the same person I was before I had children or am I an entirely new version of myself after raising my children?
And what I've come to is this.

This new chapter is not a time to wallow in who I once was but to look forward to what will be.
I am not going to ignore myself.
I am not going to ignore my own needs, my body, or my mind.
My soul has been begging me to pay attention, and this is now the time to get reacquainted with myself.

This is the time to set goals and chase after the dreams I put on hold, and this is the time to embrace all that I have done to raise four independent and confident women who walk through life with the sweetest of souls I only wish I had.

So yes, I may feel sad some days and really torn about what I miss, but I'm learning and growing once again through this process, and all I can do is embrace it.

Being a mother is about embracing and loving all of the many beautiful parts of myself that make me who I am today. It's about offering myself grace and being willing to learn new things about myself. It's being vulnerable and open to new experiences while also never letting go of the past.

Reflection

The new me is...

The Way Back Home

When I was growing up, a porch light was always left on for me, reminding me that I was home and safe. As my daughters grew up, I began to do the same. Maybe it was out of habit or maybe it was my little way of also guiding them home. But night after night as I turned the side porch light on and a golden hue in the kitchen led the way to the coziness of home and the warmth inside, I was constantly reminded of one thing. The porch light may guide the way toward home but the warmth of a mother is what truly tugs at one's heart and pulls you home.

This simple task night after night though drew me closer to my teen and connected us in a way even when we were apart. I may not know every fine detail of their life anymore, but turning the light on each night connected our hearts in a way words can't explain.

As I have gotten older, and my kids have grown, I have realized something. I want their journey toward home to always be greeted with someone waiting for them. I know this isn't always possible with raising older kids, working, and the demands of life, but if I can't be there, then the porch light can step in and be the warmth they yearn to feel as they pull up the driveway. Just as the lighthouse leads the way for sailors to find their true north, the same holds true for mothers. We lead the way for our kids offering them a light that never goes out and always guides them to the direction they need to go.

A mother's love never wavers, and the road home will always lead to an open door and arms ready to embrace our child.
A mother's love stands tall with a force that is gentle and kind, confident, and secure, ready to protect her child's heart and home.
A mother's love is irreplaceable and timeless guiding their child home to the one they call they home.
So as I continue on my journey may my girls know, that they will be always be met in the golden hue of the porch light that guides them home to me.

My soul is full when my daughter walks through the door and quietly lets out a gentle exhale feeling the comforts of home.

Reflection

Ways my love guides my big kids home...

Empty Nest

Empty nesting is my heart being swallowed up in grief.

It's a table set for two not knowing where to sit and standing, with plate in hand, wondering what this new normal will be like.

It's not rushing in the morning, but not yet knowing how to fill the morning without making lunches, waking up kids multiple times as the alarm keeps going off, and not following behind them as backpacks, keys, and coffee to-go is about to crash to the floor.

It's wandering the aisles of the grocery store, remembering all their favorite snacks and meals, but remembering not to buy so much since miles upon miles now separate us, but it's a punch to the gut each time I pick up an item out of habit and then feel an ache, letting me know, I need to put it back.

It's missing the excitement each afternoon as chaos billows in through the side door saying, "Mom, I'm home," as every fine detail of the day rushes off her lips, homework scatters the kitchen island, and snacks are consumed at a rapid pace.

It's sleeping in a dark room, which ironically keeps me awake now as the light lining the hallway, that has been on for 21 years, is now turned off and the feeling of life moving fast and childhoods gone, take over my brain as I attempt to calm myself down before laying my head on my pillow.

It's sitting on the couch alone, knowing no one is coming to sit next to me to share the latest viral recipe that we need to make, the vision board of their room, or their most precious secrets with me.

It's turning the porch light off before heading upstairs to bed knowing no one is coming home tonight and the light that always greeted them with warmth reminding them each night that loving hearts awaited them is now lighting the porch within their new home.

It's trying to find the words about the feeling of sadness taking over, but knowing there's also a beautiful journey ahead, filled with happiness and a much awaited life that has been put on hold for years. It's learning who I am again and embracing the woman and mom I am today.

It's being a mom in a different way and allowing my course to guide me where I'm supposed to be while forever being connected to my children, even though it may look different now.

It's embracing the ache yet finding hope in the beautiful gifts of tomorrow.
The gifts within the new season of empty nesting.
A season of reflection, renewal, and rebirth.

Mama, so many of us are experiencing this emotion of grief during this time. Grief isn't felt only during a death or a loss, it's a feeling many moms encounter when the house empties out and silence takes over.

Empty Nest

It's okay to grieve.
It's okay to feel it all and be sad.
It's okay to offer yourself the grace to heal as you embark on navigating this new chapter in your life.
You are not alone.
I am also swallowed up in grief learning this new normal, and you know what?
It's all going to be okay.

> *I may not understand this chapter of my life yet but one day I will and I have a feeling I'm not going to regret one minute of this part of my motherhood journey.*

Reflection

A moment while empty nesting that took my breath away...

To Go Back in Time

As my kids get older, I often wish to go back in time. It's not to relive the moment and experience it again, but to gather up every fine detail so I can hold onto it forever. It has less to do with missing a particular age but wanting to take away any mistakes I made, slow down to hug them a bit longer, and laugh with them over and over again.

This feeling has been weighing on my heart heavily these days as I watch the little girl I once knew growing up right before my eyes. I can't help but feel that a lot of moms raising teens feel this way too. But right now, I just can't stand the nostalgia and how it is tugging on every heart string holding my fragile heart together. I often get stuck in the past, holding tightly, as the looming sense of wondering if I could have done it all differently takes over my heart. Could I have done this mom gig better back then? Can I go back knowing what I know now?

Oh what I would do though to go back to those early Saturday morning birthday parties ice-skating with friends or the trips to the farm to watch the newly born baby pigs snuggle into their mother. These are the simple moments that filled up my emotional cup. Or maybe it's going back to the first time I watched my fearless daughter ski down a mountain, emanating great confidence, as she took hold of the mountain with musicality and grace I only wish I had at her age.

But I would give anything to even go back to those moments I felt sucked dry, where the weight of the world was hanging on my shoulders, feeling like a mom who didn't have enough patience or understanding.

The time I may have been too quick to say something about the outfit she was wearing as she walked down the stairs, enthusiastic, and ready to show me with pride. Or maybe when we had an argument over something simple where my filter was lost, hoping that she offered forgiveness and the wound that I caused was healed.

Mama, I think there is one common denominator we all carry around within us as mothers.
We all worry.
We all make mistakes.
We all hold on, we let go, we perseverate.
We try to make changes and learn from our mistakes.
We are mothers who understand the depth of what it means to be needed and loved and we are all mothers who know how to love with a fierce intensity.
We are moms who love hard and then love some more.

I can only imagine, as my motherhood journey takes me to many more new chapters, that my heart and mind will always yearn to wander back down memory lane. Because down that road is where all of the heartfelt moments of my life were created. All of the hardships, triumphs, tribulations, and moments that took my breath away took place down that road. A road I will never forget, forever hold onto, and always silently say a prayer of thanks. Because being a mom will always and forever be my greatest blessing.

One of the hardest things as a mother is loving my child so much that I have to let go so they can bloom and become who they need to be.

Reflection

A few ways I'm holding on while letting go. . .

Coming Home

As I gaze out my window and listen to the birds slowly appear after the long winter, I can't help but be reminded that my motherhood journey changes and evolves seasonally as well. It's not by chance that a spring emergence happens for me each and every year as the birds begin to chirp, the days get longer, and the warmth of the sun allows new buds to appear. So as I open the door into the most intimate parts of my life and reflect on my motherhood's bumpy and unpredictable road, I allow myself time to reflect during this season of new beginnings.

This is a time for new opportunities to bloom and deep reflection on how far I have grown. As I silently sip my coffee, overflowing with foamy milk to fill my soul, I will continue to be honest, transparent, and blossom into who I am meant to be at this moment in time.

Because you see, Mama, it's not just our kids growing up before our eyes.
We are also growing up alongside them as we navigate our motherhood journey.

A journey that has ebbed and flowed throughout the years with numerous twists and turns, which have caused me to also evolve and change. It's not just them growing but it's me growing up alongside them as well.

I have changed.
I am not the same woman I was before I had children.
I have grown.
I have evolved.

I am not the same woman I was before my eldest was placed in my arms that early Sunday morning. I used to be a woman carelessly frolicking about life, not knowing where I was going or how I would get there.

Mama, maybe you have changed too.
Maybe you feel the push and pull of motherhood while gripping tightly to what once was.
Maybe you also get lost in nostalgia recalling all of the bittersweet moments as your kids grew up alongside you.
And maybe your heart is also feeling weighed down by the emotional toll that evolving as a mother during this season of life entails.

The unpredictability of motherhood has deepened me in ways I never thought were possible, and as challenging as it is at times, I still wouldn't change it for a moment.

As my kids are growing up, leaving for college, entering new jobs, and even living on their own in other countries, I need to get reacquainted with the woman I am today while not forgetting who I used to be and rather merge both worlds.

I need to reintroduce myself to the woman I have always been, while merging with the woman I am today.
I need to get reacquainted with the woman I was before my greatest blessings arrived and embrace her in love.

I need to nourish her, love her, and validate who she is but I also need to allow the new me to collide with the old and embrace parts of myself as a whole.

But I can't help but feel that this season is heavy and maybe you are feeling this heaviness and weight as well.

It feels arduous and I often feel a profound ache in my heart.
Is it because my home will feel empty when my kids live miles away?
Is it because as much as letting go is necessary, it's still daunting?
Is it because I let go of my needs for so many years to fulfill the needs of my family and I need to find myself again?

All of this may be true, but I also know this to be true.
I can allow myself to sit in this reflection for some time and not get sucked down the rabbit hole of doubt, knowing my renewal and rebirth are right around the corner.

I know this is my time to reconnect with myself and recover all those parts of me that I let go of while raising my children.
It's a time to bring those passions I buried for so long to life.
It's a time to rekindle and reignite what I let burn out.

So Mamas, as the peepers emerge to sing their tune and the birds slowly begin to return, reminding me that spring is near, I will continue to uncover parts of myself that I'm just learning about.

I encourage you to also find the authentic woman who lives within the title of mom that you hold so dear to your heart. You are now a woman who is wiser, older, and filled with life's lessons within the many chapters of your life.

As I embark on my new journey, maybe a little scared, I know that I also have so much to offer as the mother I am becoming.
This new season of life may be filled with uncertainty and doubt, but there is hope for where I am headed.
Just as the birds fly south for winter and return home for spring, I too, will return home.
Home to who I have always been.
Home to who I am now.
And home to who I am becoming.

Through the many peaks and valleys, my motherhood journey will take me on, I will always return home and for that, I am forever grateful.

> *Erasing the line of who I am today and who I was prior to having children and merging both together has been one of the greatest blessings I have ever offered to myself as a woman and a mother.*

Reflection

Simple ways I'm evolving as a woman and as a mom...

Am I a perfect mother?

No.
But one thing I know for sure is this. . .
No one loves my kids more than I do.

How long will I love you? For a lifetime and beyond, forever and a day, today, and tomorrow, forever and always.

Acknowledgments

To my husband:
The man who has always told me to reach for my dreams and never give up. I am eternally grateful for your encouraging words, unwavering support, and countless forehead kisses. May our next journey be filled with more love than we can even imagine.

To my parents and sisters:
How lucky am I? Each day with you is truly a gift.

To my agent, Alex, at The Bindery:
Thank you for believing in my words and taking a chance on me. It means more than I can ever find the words for.

To Amy, Sophie, and Christine at Jossey-Bass Publishing:
Your belief in my words and enthusiasm kept me going! Thank you for the check-ins and patience throughout this process. Writing a book is not for the faint of heart, but you made it easy. I couldn't be more grateful for the role each of you played in making this dream a reality. Thank you.

To the Mamas:
I will forever be grateful for your love and support. From my heart to yours. Thank you.

About the Author

Ali Flynn is a prolific writer, speaker, influencer, certified special education teacher, and the voice behind the popular blog and website Hang in There, Mama. Ali's passion is sharing raw and vulnerable stories about raising four daughters so other moms feel less alone as they navigate their journey.